ARCHIBALD MAULE RAMSAY

THE NAMELESS WAR
The jewish power against the nations

ARCHIBALD HENRY MAULE RAMSAY
(1894-1955)

A. M. Ramsay was a British army officer who later entered politics as a Scottish Unionist MP. In 1940, after his involvement with an alleged spy in the U.S. Embassy, he became the only British MP to be interned under Defence Regulation 18B.

THE NAMELESS WAR
the jewish power against the nations

First edition, Britons Publishing Company, London - 1952

© Omnia Veritas Limited – 2021

Published by
OMNIA VERITAS LTD

www.omnia-veritas.com

All rights reserved. No part of this publication may be reproduced by any means without the prior permission of the publisher. The intellectual property code prohibits copies or reproductions for collective use. Any representation or reproduction in whole or in part by any means whatsoever, without the consent of the publisher, is unlawful and constitutes an infringement punishable by copyright laws.

INTRODUCTION 13

THE NAMELESS WAR 13

DEDICATION 17
PROLOGUE 19
THE BRITISH REVOLUTION 21
THE FRENCH REVOLUTION 35
THE RUSSIAN REVOLUTION 55

U.S.S.R. *60*
POLAND *61*
HUNGARY *61*
ROUMANIA *61*
YUGOSLAVIA *61*

DEVELOPMENT OF REVOLUTIONARY TECHNIQUE 65
GERMANY BELLS THE CAT 73
1933: JEWRY DECLARES WAR 81
"PHONEY WAR" ENDED BY CIVILIAN BOMBING 93
DUNKIRK AND AFTER 99
THE SHAPE OF THINGS TO COME 103
PRESIDENT ROOSEVELT'S ROLE 107
REGULATION 18B 115
WHO DARES? 121
EPILOGUE 127
STATEMENT 133

Statement by Capt. Ramsay from Brixton Prison to the Speaker and Members of Parliament concerning his detention under Paragraph 18B of the Defence Regulations *133*
PHASE I *134*
PHASE II *134*

PARTICULARS ALLEGED AS REASONS FOR MY DETENTION **151**

PARTICULARS 152

CONCLUSION **163**
THE STATUTES OF JEWRY **165**

THE STATUTES OF JEWRY 165

THE JEWS IN BRITAIN **171**
FAMOUS MEN ON THE JEWS **173**
COPY OF LEAFLET DESIGNED BY THE AUTHOR AFTER THE MUNICH AGREEMENT **177**

GERMAN WHITE BOOK ON THE LAST PHASE OF THE GERMAN-POLISH CRISIS 180
THE LAST PHASE OF THE GERMAN-POLISH CRISIS 187

OTHER TITLES **197**

Captain Archibald Maule Ramsay was educated at Eton and the Royal Military College, Sandhurst, and served with the 2nd Battalion Coldstream Guards in the First World War until he was severely wounded in 1916 - thereafter at Regimental H.Q. and the War Office and the British War Mission in Paris until the end of the war.

From 1920 he became a Member of H.M. Scottish Bodyguard. In 1931 he was elected a Member of Parliament for Midlothian and Peeblesshire.

Arrested under Regulation 18b on the 23rd May, 1940, he was detained, without charge or trial, in a cell in Brixton Prison until the 26th September, 1944. On the following morning he resumed his seat in the House of Commons and remained there until the end of that Parliament in 1945.

A. M. RAMSAY

INTRODUCTION

THE NAMELESS WAR

Here is the story that people have said would never be written in our time - the true history of events leading up to the Second World War, told by one who enjoyed the friendship and confidence of Mr Neville Chamberlain during the critical months between Munich and September, 1939.

There has long been an unofficial ban on books dealing with what Captain Ramsay calls "The Nameless War", the conflict which has been waged from behind the political scene for centuries, which is still being waged and of which very few are aware.

The publishers of "The Nameless War" believe this latest exposure will do more than any previous attempt to break the conspiracy of silence.

The present work, with much additional evidence and a fuller historical background, is the outcome of the personal experiences of a public figure who in the course of duty has discovered at first-hand the existence of a centuries old conspiracy against Britain, Europe, and the whole of Christendom.

"The Nameless War" reveals an unsuspected link between all the major revolutions in Europe - from King Charles I's time to the abortive attempt against Spain in 1936. One source of inspiration, design and supply is shown to be common to all of them. These revolutions and the World War of 1939 are seen to be integral parts of one and the same master plan.

After a brief review of the forces behind the declaration of war and the world wide arrests of many who endeavoured to oppose them, the author describes the anatomy of the Revolutionary International machine - the machine which today continues the plan for supranational world power, the age-old Messianic dream of International Jewry.

It is the author's belief that the machine would break down without the support of its unwilling Jews and unsuspecting Gentiles and he puts forward suggestions for detaching these elements.

Christians say:

> "Captain Ramsay, a Christian gentleman of unflagging courage, believed that the war with Germany was not conceived in the interests of Britain and could lead only to the extension of Communist and Jewish power. Because he warned his fellow countrymen of the forces at work, he was put in prison without trial for four and a half years, for 'reasons' so preposterous that those who framed them dared not submit them to a court of law."

Truth

> "For years Captain Ramsay had been a member of the

British Parliament. His book is an analysis of the Jewish-Zionist war against Christian civilization."

The Cross and the Flag

Jews say:

"There is no limit to the depths of human depravity; Captain Maule Ramsay seems to have made a very determined attempt to plumb those depths."

The Jewish Chronicle

"The publication of such a book, at this time, underlines the urgent need for the law to be reformed so as to make it a crime to preach racial hatred or publish libels on groups in the community."

The Daily Worker

A. M. RAMSAY

DEDICATION

To the memory of those Patriots who in 1215 at Runnymede signed Magna Carta and those who in 1320 at Arbroath signed the Declaration of Independence this book is dedicated.

27th July 1952

A. M. RAMSAY

PROLOGUE

Edward I banished the Jews from England for many grave offences endangering the welfare of his realm and lieges, which were to a great extent indicated in the Statutes of Jewry [1], enacted by his Parliament in 1290, the Commons playing a prominent part.

The King of France very shortly followed suit, as did other Rulers in Christian Europe. So grave did the situation for the Jews in Europe become, that an urgent appeal for help and advice was addressed by them to the Sanhedrin, then located at Constantinople.

This appeal was sent over the signature of Chemor, Rabbi of Arles in Provence, on the 13th January, 1489. The reply came in November, 1489, which was issued over the signature of V.S.S. V.F.F. Prince of the Jews.

It advised the Jews of Europe to adopt the tactics of the Trojan Horse; to make their sons Christian priests, lawyers, doctors, etc., and work to destroy the Christian structure from within.

The first notable repercussion to this advice occurred in

---

[1] See Appendix 2 (Appendices follow the last chapter)

Spain in the reign of Ferdinand and Isabella. Many Jews were by then enrolled as Christians, but remaining secretly Jews were working to destroy the Christian church in Spain.

So grave became the menace finally, that the Inquisition was instituted in an endeavour to cleanse the country from these conspirators. Once again the Jews were compelled to commence an exodus from yet another country, whose hospitality they had abused.

Trekking eastwards, these Jews joined other Jewish communities in Western Europe; considerable numbers flowed on to Holland and Switzerland.

From now on these two countries were to become active centres of Jewish intrigue. Jewry, however, has always needed a powerful seafaring nation to which to attach itself.

Great Britain, newly united under James I, was a rising naval power, which was already beginning to sway the four corners of the discovered world. Here also there existed a wonderful field for disruptive criticism; for although it was a Christian kingdom, yet it was one most sharply divided as between Protestant and Catholic.

A campaign for exploiting this division and fanning hatreds between the Christian communities was soon in process of organization. How well the Jews succeeded in this campaign in Britain may be judged from the fact that one of the earliest acts of their creature and hireling Oliver Cromwell - after executing the King according to plan - was to allow the Jews free access to England once more.

THE BRITISH REVOLUTION

"It was fated that England should be the first of a series of Revolutions, which is not yet finished."

With these cryptic words Isaac Disraeli, father of Benjamin Earl of Beaconsfield, commenced his two volume life of Charles I published in 1851. A work of astonishing detail and insight, much information for which, he states, was obtained from the records of one Melchior de Salom, French envoy in England during that period.

The scene opens with distant glimpses of the British Kingdom based upon Christianity, and its own ancient traditions; these sanctions binding Monarchy, Church, State, nobles and the people in one solemn bond on the one hand; on the other hand, the ominous rumblings of Calvinism.

Calvin, who came to Geneva from France, where his name was spelt Cauin[2], possibly a French effort to spell Cohen, organized great numbers of revolutionary orators, not a few of whom were inflicted upon England and Scotland. Thus was laid the groundwork for

---

[2] At a B'nai B'rith meeting in Paris reported in 'Catholic Gazette' in Feb 1936 he was claimed to be of Jewish extraction.

revolution under a cloak of religious fervour.

On both sides of the Tweed these demagogues contracted all religion into rigid observance of the "Sabbath." To use the words of Isaac Disraeli:

> "The nation was artfully divided into Sabbatarians and Sabbath breakers." "Calvin deemed the Sabbath to have been a Jewish ordinance, limited to the sacred people."

He goes on to say that when these Calvinists held the country in their power:

> "It seemed that religion chiefly consisted of Sabbatarian rigours; and that a British senate had been transformed into a company of Hebrew Rabbins."

And later:

> "In 1650, after the execution of the King, an Act was passed inflicting penalties for a breach of the Sabbath."

Buckingham, Strafford and Laud are the three chief figures round the King in these early stages: Men on whose loyalty to himself, the nation, and the ancient tradition Charles can rely.

Buckingham, the trusted friend of King James I, and of those who had saved his life at the time of the Gowrie Conspiracy (of ominous cabalistic associations) was assassinated in the early years of King Charles' reign under mysterious circumstances.

Strafford, who had been in his early days inclined to follow the opposite faction, later left them; and became a staunch and devoted adherent of the King.

This opposition faction became steadily more hostile to Charles and by the time that they were led by Pym and decided to impeach Strafford. "The King", writes Disraeli, "regarded this faction as his enemies"; and he states that the head of this faction was the Earl of Bedford.

Walsh, the eminent Catholic historian, states that a Jew wine merchant named Roussel was the founder of this family in Tudor times. With the impeachment and execution of Strafford, the powers behind the rising Calvinist, or Cohenist, Conspiracy began to reveal themselves, and their focus, the City of London.

At this time there suddenly began to appear from the City armed mobs of "Operatives" (the medieval equivalent for "workers" no doubt). Let me quote Disraeli:

> "They were said to amount to ten thousand ... with warlike weapons. It was a militia for insurgency at all seasons, and might be depended upon for any work of destruction at the cheapest rate ... as these sallied forth with daggers and bludgeons (from the city) the inference is obvious that this train of explosion must have been long laid."

It must indeed; and we must recollect here, that at this time Strafford was still unexecuted, and civil war in the minds of none but of those behind the scenes, who evidently had long since resolved upon and planned it.

These armed mobs of "workers" intimidated all and sundry, including both Houses of Parliament and the

Palace at critical moments, exactly on the model employed later by the "Sacred Bands" and the "Marseillais" in the French Revolution.

Isaac Disraeli draws again and again startling parallels between this and the French Revolution; Notably in his passages on the **Press, "no longer under restraint,"** and the deluge of revolutionary pamphlets and leaflets. He writes:

> "From 1640 to 1660, about 30,000 appear to have started up."

And later:

> "The collection of French revolutionary pamphlets now stands by the side of the French tracts of the age of Charles I, as abundant in number and as fierce in passion… Whose hand behind the curtain played the strings… could post up a correct list of 59 commoners, branding them with the odious title of 'Straffordians' or betrayers of their country."

Whose hand indeed? But Disraeli who knew so much, now discreetly draws a veil over that iron curtain; and it is left to us to complete the revelation.

To do so we must turn to such other works as the Jewish Encyclopaedia, Sombart's work, The Jews and Modern Capitalism, and others. From these we learn that Cromwell, the chief figure of the revolution, was in close contact with the powerful Jew financiers in Holland; and was in fact paid large sums of money by Manasseh Ben Israel; whilst Fernandez Carvajal, "The Great Jew" as he was called, was the chief contractor of the New Model Army.

In *The Jews in England* we read:

> "1643 brought a large contingent of Jews to England, their rallying point was the house of the Portuguese Ambassador De Souza, a Marrano (secret Jew). Prominent among them was Fernandez Carvajal, a great financier and army contractor."

In January of the previous year, the attempted arrest of the five members had set in violent motion the armed gangs of "Operatives" already mentioned, from the city. Revolutionary pamphlets were broadcasted on this occasion, as Disraeli tells us:

> "Bearing the ominous insurrectionary cry of 'To your tents, O Israel'."

Shortly after this the King and the Royal Family left the Palace of Whitehall.

The five members with armed mobs and banners accompanying them, were given a triumphal return to Westminster. The stage was now set for the advent of Carvajal and his Jews and the rise of their creature Cromwell.

The scene now changes. The Civil War has taken its course. The year is 1647: Naseby has been won and lost. The King is virtually a prisoner, while treated as an honoured guest at Holmby House.

According to a letter published in *Plain English* (a weekly review published by the North British Publishing Co. and edited by the late Lord Alfred Douglas.) on 3rd September, 1921:

"The Learned Elders have been in existence for a much longer period than they have perhaps suspected. My friend, Mr. L. D. van Valckert, of Amsterdam, has recently sent me a letter containing two extracts from the Synagogue at Mulheim. The volume in which they are contained was lost at some period during the Napoleonic Wars, and has recently come into Mr. van Valckert's possession. It is written in German, and contains extracts of letters sent and received by the authorities of the Mulheim Synagogue. The first entry he sends me is of a letter received:

16th June, 1647

From O.C. (i.e. Oliver Cromwell), by Ebenezer Pratt.

In return for financial support will advocate admission of Jews to England: This however impossible while Charles living.

Charles cannot be executed without trial, adequate grounds for which do not at present exist. Therefore advise that Charles be assassinated, but will have nothing to do with arrangements for procuring an assassin, though willing to help in his escape.

In reply was dispatched the following:

12th July, 1647

To O.C. by E. Pratt.

Will grant financial aid as soon as Charles removed and Jews admitted. Assassination too

> *dangerous. Charles shall be given opportunity to escape: His recapture will make trial and execution possible. The support will be liberal, but useless to discuss terms until trial commences.*

With this information now at our disposal, the subsequent moves on the part of the regicides stand out with a new clearness. On 4th June, 1647, Cornet Joyce, acting on secret orders from Cromwell himself, and, according to Disraeli, unknown even to General-in-Chief Fairfax, descended upon Holmby House with 500 picked revolutionary troopers, and seized the King. According to Disraeli:

> "The plan was arranged on May 30th at a secret meeting held at Cromwell's house, though later Cromwell pretending that it was without his concurrence."

This move coincided with a sudden development in the army; the rise of the 'Levelers' and "Rationalists." Their doctrines were those of the French revolutionaries; in fact, what we know today as Communism. These were the regicides, who four times "purged" Parliament, till there was left finally 50 members, Communist-like themselves, known later as the Rump.

To return to the letter from Mulheim Synagogue of the 12th June, 1647, and its cunning suggestion that attempted escape should be used as a pretext for execution. Just such an event took place, on 12th November of that year. Hollis and Ludlow consider the flight as a stratagem of Cromwell's. Isaac Disraeli states:

> "Contemporary historians have decided that the King

from the day of his deportation from Holmby to his escape to the Isle of Wight was throughout the dupe of Cromwell."

Little more remains to be said. Cromwell had carried out the orders from the Synagogue, and now it only remained to stage the mock trial.

Maneuvering for position continued for some time. And it became apparent that the House of Commons, even in their partially "purged" condition, were in favour of coming to an agreement with the King. On 5th December 1648, the House sat all night; and finally carried the question, "That the King's concessions were satisfactory to a settlement."

Should such agreement have been reached, of course, Cromwell would not have received the large sums of money which he was hoping to get from the Jews. He struck again. On the night of December 6th, Colonel Pryde, on his instructions, carried out the last and most famous "purge" of the House of Commons, known as "Pryde's Purge."

On 4th January, the Communist remnant of 50 members, the Rump, invested themselves with "the supreme authority."

On 9th January "a High Court of Justice" to try the King was proclaimed. Two-thirds of its members were Levelers from the Army. Algernon Sidney warned Cromwell: "First, the King can be tried by no court. Second, no man can be tried by this court."

So writes Hugh Ross Williamson in his *Charles and*

Cromwell; and he adds a finishing touch to the effect that "no English lawyer could be found to draw up the charge, which was eventually entrusted to an accommodating alien, Isaac Dorislaus."

Needless to say, Isaac Dorislaus was exactly the same sort of alien as Carvajal and Manasseh Ben Israel and the other financiers who paid the "Protector" his blood money.

The Jews were once again permitted to land freely in England in spite of strong protests by the sub-committee of the Council of State, which declared that they would be a grave menace to the State and the Christian religion. Perhaps it is due to their protests that the actual act of banishment has never to this day been repealed.

> "The English Revolution under Charles I was unlike any preceding one ... From that time and event we contemplate in our history the phases of revolution."

> Isaac Disraeli

There were many more to follow on similar lines, notably in France.

In 1897 a further important clue to these mysterious happenings fell into Gentile hands in the shape of the *Protocols of the Elders of Zion*. In that document we read this remarkable sentence:

> "*Remember the French Revolution, the secrets of its preparation are well known to us for it was entirely the work of our hands.*" [Protocol No.3]

The Elders might have made the passage even fuller, and written, "Remember the British and French revolutions, the secrets of which are well known to us for they were entirely the work of our hands."

The difficult problem of the subjugation of both Kingdoms was still however unsolved. Scotland was Royalist before everything else; and she had proclaimed Charles II King. Cromwell's armies marched round Scotland, aided by their Geneva sympathizers, dispensing Judaic barbarity; but Scotland still called Charles II King. He moreover accepted the Presbyterian form of Christianity for Scotland; and slowly but steadily the feeling in England began to come round to the Scottish point of view.

Finally upon the death of Cromwell, all Britain welcomed the King's restoration to the throne of England.

In 1660 Charles II returned; but there was an important difference between the Kingdom he had fled from as a boy, and the one to which he returned as King. The enemies of Kingship were entrenched within his kingdom now, and as soon as the stage should be set for renewing the propaganda against the papacy and so, dividing once more persons, all of whom considered themselves as part of Christ's Church, the next attack would develop.

The next attack would aim at placing the control of the finances of both Kingdoms in the hands of the Jews, who were now firmly ensconced within.

Charles evidently had no consciousness of the Jewish

problem or plans, or the menace they held for his peoples. The wisdom and experience of Edward I had become lost in the centuries of segregation from the Jewish virus. A consciousness of the danger to the Crown in placing his enemies in possession of the weapon of a "Popish Plot" cry he did retain.

With James II's accession, the crisis could not be long delayed. The most unscrupulous pamphleteering and propaganda was soon in full swing against him, and it is no surprise to find that many of the vilest pamphlets were actually printed in Holland. This country was now quite openly the focus for all disaffected persons; and considerable comings and goings took place during these years.

Stories were brought to the King that his own brother-in-law had joined those who plotted against him; but he utterly refused to credit them, or take any action till news came that the expedition against himself was actually under way.

The chief figure amongst those who deserted James at that crucial juncture was John Churchill, first Duke of Marlborough. It is interesting to read in the Jewish Encyclopaedia that this Duke for many years received not less than 6,000 pounds a year from the Dutch Jew Solomon Medina.

The real objective of the "Glorious Revolution" was achieved a few years later in 1694, when the Royal consent was given for the setting up of the "Bank of England" and the institution of the National Debt.

This charter handed over to an anonymous committee the

Royal prerogative of minting money; **converted the basis of wealth to gold**; and enabled the international money lenders to secure their loans on the taxes of the country, instead of the doubtful undertaking of some ruler or potentate which was all the security they could previously obtain.

From that time economic machinery was set in motion which ultimately reduced all wealth to the **fictitious terms of gold which the Jews control**; and drained away the life blood of the land, the real wealth which was the birthright of the British peoples[3].

The political and economic union of England and Scotland was shortly afterwards forced upon Scotland with wholesale corruption, and in defiance of formal protests from every county and borough. The main objects of the Union were to suppress the Royal Mint in Scotland, and to force upon her, too, responsibility for the "National Debt."

The grip of the moneylender was now complete throughout Britain. The danger was that the members of the new joint Parliament would sooner or later, in the spirit of their ancestors, challenge this state of affairs. To provide against this, therefore, the **party system** was now brought into being, frustrating true national reaction and enabling the wire-pullers to divide and rule; using their newly-established financial power to ensure that

---

[3] Germany's most successful economic system was NOT backed by gold. He eluded the blood-sucking grip of the Zionist Jew Money Masters, therefore "Germany must be destroyed!" and Adolf Hitler vilified down through ages so the uninformed will DEMAND their government return to the gold standard.

their own men and their own policies should secure the limelight, and sufficient support from their newspapers, pamphlets, and banking accounts to carry the day.

Gold was soon to become the basis of loans, ten times the size of the amount deposited. In other words, 100 pounds in gold would be legal security for 1,000 pounds of loan; at 3% therefore 100 pounds in gold could earn 30 pounds interest annually with no more trouble to the lender than the keeping of a few ledger entries.

The owner of 100 pounds of land, however, still must work every hour of daylight in order to make perhaps 4%. The end of the process must only be a matter of time. The moneylenders must become millionaires; those who own and work the land, the Englishman and the Scotsman, must be ruined. The process has continued inexorably till now, when it is nearly completed.

It has been hypocritically camouflaged by clever propaganda as helping the poor by mulcting the rich. It has been in reality nothing of the kind. It has been in the main the deliberate ruination of the landed classes, the leaders among the Gentiles, and their supplanting by the Jew financiers and their hangers-on.

THE FRENCH REVOLUTION

The French Revolution of 1789 was the most startling event in the history of Europe since the fall of Rome.

A new phenomenon then appeared before the world. Never before had a mob apparently organized successful revolution against all other classes in the state, under high sounding, but quite nonsensical slogans, and with methods bearing not a trace of the principles enshrined in those slogans.

Never before had any one section of any nation conquered all other sections; and still less swept away every feature of the national life and tradition, from King, religion, nobles, clergy, constitution, flag, calendar, and place names, to coinage.

Such a phenomenon merits the closest attention; especially in view of the fact that it has been followed by identical outbreaks in many countries.

The main discovery that such an examination will reveal is this fact:

The revolution was not the work of Frenchmen to improve France. It was the work of aliens, whose

object was to destroy everything, which had been France.

This conclusion is borne out by the references to "foreigners" in high places in the Revolutionary Councils, not only by Sir Walter Scott, but by Robes Pierre himself.

We have the names of several of them, and it is clear that they were not British, or Germans, or Italians, or any other nationals; they were, of course, Jews.

Let us see what the Jews themselves have to say about it:

> *"Remember the French Revolution to which it was we who gave the name of 'Great.' The secrets of its preparation are well known to us for it was wholly the work of our hands."*

Protocols of Zion No. 7.

> *"We were the first to cry among the masses of the people the words 'Liberty, Equality, Fraternity.' The stupid Gentile poll parrots flew down from all sides on to these baits, and with them carried away the well-being of the world. The would-be-wise men of the Gentiles were so stupid that they could not see that in nature there is no equality, and there cannot be freedom (meaning, of course, freedom as understood by Socialists and Communists, freedom to wreck your own country)."*

Protocols of Zion-No. 1.

With this knowledge in our possession we shall find we possess a master key to the intricate happenings of the

French Revolution. The somewhat confused picture of characters and events moving across the screen, which our history books have shown us, will suddenly become a concerted and connected human drama.

When we begin to draw parallels between France of 1789, Britain of 1640, Russia of 1917, Germany and Hungary of 1918-19, and Spain of 1936, we shall feel that drama grip us with a new and personal sense of reality.

"Revolution is a blow struck at a paralytic."

Even so, however, it must be obvious that immense organization, and vast resources, as well as cunning and secrecy far above the ordinary are necessary for its successful preparation.

It is amazing indeed that people should suppose that "mobs" or "the people" ever have, or ever could, undertake such a complicated and costly operation. No mistake more-over could be more dangerous; for it will result in total inability to recognize the true significance of events, or the source and focus of a revolutionary movement.

The process or organizing revolution is seen to be **firstly the infliction of paralysis; and secondly, the striking of the blow or blows.** It is for the first process, the production of paralysis, that the secrecy is essential. Its outward signs are debt, loss of publicity control, and the **existence of alien- influenced secret organizations in the doomed state.**

Debt, particularly international debt, **is the first and**

over-mastering grip. Through it men in high places are suborned and alien powers and influences are introduced into the body politic. When the debt grip has been firmly established, control of every form of publicity and political activity soon follows, together with a full grip on industrialists.

The stage for the revolutionary blow is then set. The grip of the right hand of finance established the paralysis; while it is the revolutionary left that holds the dagger and deals the fatal blow. Moral corruption facilitates the whole process.

By 1780 financial paralysis was making its appearance in France. The world's big financiers were firmly established.

> "They possessed so large a share of the world's gold and silver stocks, that they had most of Europe in their debt, certainly France."

So writes Mr McNair Wilson in his *Life of Napoleon*, and continues on page 38:

> "A change of a fundamental kind had taken place in the economic structure of Europe whereby the old basis had ceased to be wealth and had become debt. In the old Europe wealth had been measured in lands, crops, herds and minerals; but a new standard had now been introduced, namely, a form of money to which the title 'credit' had been given."

The debts of the French Kingdom though substantial were by no means insurmountable, except in terms of gold: and had the King's advisers decided to issue money on the security of the lands and real wealth of France, the position could have been fairly easily righted. As it was the situation was firmly gripped by one financier after another, who either could not or would not break with the system imposed by the international usurers.

Under such weakness, or villainy, the bonds of usury could only grow heavier and more terrible, for debts were in terms of gold or silver, neither of which France produced.

And who were the potentates of the new debt machine; these manipulators of gold and silver, who had succeeded in turning upside down the finances of Europe, and replacing real wealth by millions upon millions of usurious loans?

The late Lady Queensborough, in her important work *Occult Theocracy* gives us certain outstanding names, taking her facts from *L'Anti-Semitisme* by the Jew Bernard Lazare, 1894.

In London she gives the names of Benjamin Goldsmid and his brother Abraham Goldsmid, Moses Mocatta their partner, and his nephew Sir Moses Montifiore, as being directly concerned in financing the French Revolution, along with Daniel Itsig of Berlin and his son-in-law David Friedlander, and Herz Cerfbeer of Alsace. These names recall the *Protocols of Zion*, and turning up Number 20 we read:

> "The gold standard has been the ruin of States which adopted it, for it has not been able to satisfy the demands for money, the more so as we have removed gold from circulation as far as possible."

And Again:

> "Loans hang like a Sword of Damocles over the heads of rulers who come begging with outstretched palm."

No words could describe more aptly what was overtaking France. Sir Walter Scott in his *Life of Napoleon*, Vol. 1, thus describes the situation:

> "These financiers used the government as bankrupt prodigals are treated by usurious moneylenders, who feeding their extravagance with the one hand, with the other wring out of their ruined fortunes the most unreasonable recompenses for their advances. By a long succession of these ruinous loans, and the various rights granted to guarantee them, the whole finances of France were brought to total confusion."

King Louis' chief finance minister during these last years of growing confusion was Necker, "a Swiss" of German extraction, son of a German professor of whom McNair Wilson writes:

> "Necker had forced his way into the King's Treasury as a representative of the debt system owning allegiance to that system."

We can easily imagine what policy that allegiance inspired in Necker; and when we add to this the fact that his previous record was that of a daring and unscrupulous speculator, we can understand why the national finances of France under his baneful aegis rapidly worsened, so that after four years of his manipulations, the unfortunate King's government had contracted an additional and far more serious debt of 170,000,000 pounds.

By 1730 Freemasonry had been introduced into France from England. By 1771 the movement had attained such proportions that Philippe Duc de Chartres afterwards d'Orléans became Grand Master. This type of freemasonry was largely innocent, both in policy and personnel in its early days; but as events proved, the real moving spirits were ruthless and unscrupulous men of blood.

The Duc d'Orléans was not one of these latter. Though a man of little principle, and an extravagant, vain and ambitious libertine, he had no motives beyond the ousting of the King, and the establishing of a democratic monarchy with himself as that monarch.

Having in addition but little intelligence, he made the ideal stalking horse for the first and most moderate stage of revolution, and a willing tool of men whom he probably scarcely knew; and who **sent him to the guillotine soon after his base and ignominious role had been played**.

The Marquis de Mirabeau who succeeded him as the leading figure of the Revolution was cast in much the same role. He was a much abler man than d'Orléans, but so foul a libertine that he was shunned by all his own class, and imprisoned more than once at the instance of his own father. He is known to have been financed by Moses Mendelssohn[4], head of the Jewish Illuminati, and to have been more in the company of the Jewess Mrs.

---

[4] Moses Mendelssohn is the 'learned Jew' who is quoted as saying that: "Judaism is not a religion. It is a law religionized." To my mind, that is the same as saying that "Judaism is a political program (for World Dominion) wrapped in a cloak of religion".

Herz than was her husband. He was not only an early figure-head in French Freemasonry in the respectable years, but introduced Illuminism into France.

This Illuminism was a secret revolutionary society behind freemasonry. The Illuminati penetrated into all the lodges of Grand Orient Freemasonry, and were backed and organized by cabalistic Jews.

It is interesting to note that the Duc D'Orléans and Talleyrand were both initiated into Illuminism by Mirabeau shortly after the latter had introduced it into France, from Frankfurt, where its headquarters had been established in 1782 under Adam Weishaupt.

In 1785 there happened a strange event, which makes it seem as though the heavenly powers themselves made a last moment attempt to warn France and Europe against these massing powers of evil:

Lightning struck dead a messenger of the Illuminati at Ratisbon.

The police found on the body papers dealing with plans for world revolution.

Thereupon the Bavarian Government had the headquarters of the Illuminati searched, and much further evidence was discovered.

French authorities were informed, but **the process of paralysis was too far advanced, and no action resulted**.

By 1789 there were more than two thousand Lodges in

France affiliated to the Grand Orient, the direct tool of international revolution; and their adepts numbered over 100,000. Thus we get Jewish Illuminism under Moses Mendelssohn and Masonic Illuminism under Weishaupt established as the inner controls of a strong secret organization covering the whole of France.

Under the Illuminati worked Grand Orient Freemasonry, and under that again the Blue, or National, Masonry had operated until it was converted over-night into Grand Orient Masonry by Philippe d'Orléans in 1773. Little did Égalité suspect the satanic powers that he was invoking, when he took that action, and satanic they certainly were. The name Lucifer means "Light Bearer"; and Illuminati those who were lit by that light.

By the time the Estates General met at Versailles on 5th May, 1789, the paralysis of the executive authority by the secret organizations was complete. Paralysis by control of public opinion and publicity was well advanced by then also. This was the manner of its accomplishment.

By 1780 d'Orléans' entire income of 800,000 livres, thanks to his reckless gambling and extravagance, was mortgaged to the moneylenders.

In 1781, in return for accommodation, he signed papers handing over his palace, estates, and house the Palais Royal, to his creditors, with powers to form there a centre of politics, printing, pamphleteering, gambling, lectures, brothels, wine-shops, theatres, art galleries, athletics, and any other uses, which subsequently took the form of every variety of public debauchery.

In fact, Égalité's financial masters used his name and

property to install a colossal organism for publicity and corruption, which appealed to every lowest instinct in human nature; and deluged the enormous crowds so gathered with the filthy, defamatory and revolutionary output of its printing presses and debating clubs.

As Scudder writes in *A Prince of the Blood*:

> "It gave the police more to do than all the other parts of the city."

It is interesting to note that the general manager installed by the creditors at the Palais royal was one de Laclos, a political adventurer of alien origin, author of *Liaisons Dangereuses,* and other pornographic works, who was said "to study the politics of love because of his love for politics."

This steady stream of corruption and destructive propaganda was linked with a series of systematic personal attacks of the vilest and most unscrupulous nature upon any public characters whom the Jacobins thought likely to stand in their way. This process was known as "L'infamie."

Marie Antoinette herself was one of the chief targets for this typically Jewish form of attack. No lie or abuse was too vile to level at her. More intelligent, alert, and vigorous than the weak and indolent Louis, Marie Antoinette presented a considerable obstacle to the revolution. She had, more-over, received many warnings regarding freemasonry from her sister in Austria; and no doubt was by this time more awake to its significance than when she had written to her sister some years previously:

"I believe that as far as France is concerned, you worry too much about freemasonry. Here it is far from having the significance that it may have elsewhere in Europe. Here everything is open and one knows all. Then where could the danger be?

One might well be worried if it were a question of a political secret society. But on the contrary the government lets it spread, and it is only that which it seems, an association the objects of which are union and charity.

One dines, one sings, one talks, which has given the King occasion to say that people who drink and sing are not suspect of organizing plots. Nor is it a society of atheists, for we are told God is on the lips of all. They are very charitable. They bring up the children of their poor and dead members. They endow their daughters. What harm is there in all that?"

What harm indeed if these blameless pretensions masked no darker designs? Doubtless the agents of Weishaupt and Mendelssohn reported on to them the contents of the Queen's letter; and we can imagine them shaking with laughter, and rubbing their hands in satisfaction; hands that were itching to destroy the very life of France and her Queen; and which at the appropriate hour would give the signal that would convert secret conspiracy into the "massacres of September" and the blood baths of the guillotine.

In order to further the campaign of calumny against the Queen, an elaborate hoax was arranged at the time, when the financiers and grain speculators were deliberately creating conditions of poverty and hunger in Paris.

A diamond necklace valued at nearly a quarter of a million was ordered at the Court jewellers in the Queen's name by an agent of the Jacobins. The unfortunate Queen knew nothing of this affair until the necklace was brought round to her for acceptance, when she naturally disclaimed anything to do with the matter, pointing out that she would consider it wrong to order such a thing when France was in so bad a financial way.

The printing presses of the Palais Royal, however, turned full blast on to the subject; and every kind of criticism levelled at the Queen.

A further scandal was then engineered for the presses. Some prostitute from the Palais Royal was engaged to disguise herself as the Queen; and by the forged letter the Cardinal Prince de Rohan was induced to meet the supposed Queen about midnight at the Palais Royal, supposing he was being asked for advice and help by the Queen on the subject of the necklace.

This event, needless to say, was immediately reported to the printing presses and pamphleteers, who started a further campaign containing the foulest innuendoes that could be imagined concerning the whole affair. The moving spirit behind the scene was Cagliostro, alias Joseph Balsamo, a Jew from Palermo, a doctor of the cabalistic art, and a member of the Illuminati, into which he was initiated at Frankfurt by Weishaupt in 1774.

When the necklace had finally served its purpose, it was sent over to London, where most of the stones were retained by the Jew Eliason. Attacks of a similar nature were directed against many other decent people, who resisted the influence of the Jacobin clubs. After eight years of this work the process of paralysis by mastery of publicity was complete.

In every respect therefore by 1789, when the financiers forced the King to summon the Estates General, the first portion of their plans for revolution (i.e. paralysis) were accomplished. It now only remained to strike the blow or series of blows, which were to rob France of her throne, her church, her constitution, her nobles, her clergy, her gentry, her bourgeoisie, her traditions, and her culture; leaving in their place, when the guillotine's work was done, citizen hewers of wood and drawers of water under an alien financial dictatorship.

From 1789 onwards a succession of revolutionary acts were set in motion; each more violent than the one preceding it; each unmasking fresh demands and more violent and revolutionary leaders. In their turn each of these leaders, a puppet only of the real powers behind the revolution, is set aside; and his head rolls into the basket to join those of his victims of yesterday.

Philippe Égalité, Duc d'Orléans, was used to prepare the ground for the revolution; to protect with his name and influence the infancy of the revolutionary club; to popularize freemasonry and the Palais Royal; and to sponsor such acts as the march of the women to Versailles.

The "women" on this occasion were mostly men in disguise. D'Orléans was under the impression that the King and Queen would be assassinated by this mob, and himself proclaimed a democratic King. The real planners of the march, however, had other schemes in view.

One main objective was to secure the removal of the royal family to Paris, where they would be clear of protection from the army, and under the power of the Commune or Paris County Council in which the Jacobins were supreme.

They continued to make use of Égalité right up to the time of the vote on the King's life, when he crowned his sordid career by leading the open vote in voting for the death of his cousin. His masters thereafter had no further use for his services; and he very shortly followed his cousin to the guillotine amidst the execrations of all classes.

Mirabeau played a similar role to that of Égalité. He had intended that the revolution should cease with the setting up of Louis as a democratic monarch with himself as chief adviser. He had no desire to see violence done to the King. On the contrary, in the last days before he died mysteriously by poison, he exerted all his efforts to get the King removed from Paris, and placed in charge of loyal generals still commanding his army.

He was the last of the moderates and monarchists to dominate the Jacobin club of Paris; that bloodthirsty focus of revolution, which had materialized out of the secret clubs of the Orient Masons and Illuminati. It was Mirabeau's voice, loud and resonant, that kept in check the growing rage of the murderous fanatics who swarmed therein.

There is no doubt that he perceived at last the true nature and strength of the beast, which he had worked so long and so industriously to unchain. In his last attempt to save the royal family by getting them out of Paris, he actually succeeded in shouting down all opposition in the Jacobin club. That evening he died by a sudden and violent illness; and, as the author of *The Diamond Necklace* writes:

> "Louis was not ignorant that Mirabeau had been poisoned."

Thus, like Philippe Égalité, and later Danton and Robespierre, Mirabeau too was removed from the stage when his role had been played. We are reminded of the passage in Number 15 of the *Protocols of Zion*:

> *"We execute masons in such wise that none save the brotherhood can ever have a suspicion of it."*

And again:

> *"In this way we shall proceed with those goy masons who know too much."*

As Mr E. Scudder writes in his *Life of Mirabeau*:

> *"He died at a moment when the revolution might still have been checked."*

The figure of Lafayette occupies the stage on several important occasions during these first revolutionary stages. He was one of those simple freemasons, who are borne they know not wither, in a ship they have not fully explored, and by currents concerning which they are totally ignorant.

While a popular figure with the revolutionary crowds, he very severely handled several incipient outbreaks of revolutionary violence, notably in the march of the women to Versailles, during the attack on the Tuileries, and at the Champs de Mars. He, too, desired the establishment of a democratic monarchy, and would countenance no threat to the King even from Philippe Égalité, whom he treated with the utmost hostility during and after the march of the women to Versailles, believing on that occasion that Égalité intended the assassination of the King, and the usurpation of the Crown.

He evidently became an obstacle to the powers behind the revolution, and was packed off to a war against Austria, which the Assembly forced Louis to declare. Once he did dash back to Paris in an effort to save the King; but he was packed off again to the war. Mirabeau's death followed, and Louis' fate was sealed.

The wild figures of Danton, Marat, Robespierre, and the fanatics of the Jacobin club now dominated the scene.

In September of 1792 were perpetrated the terrible "September massacres"; 8,000 persons being murdered in the prisons of Paris alone, and many more over the country.

It should be noted here, that these victims were arrested and held till the time of the massacre in the prisons by one Manuel, Procurer of the Commune. Sir Walter Scott evidently understood much concerning the influences which were at work behind the scenes. In his *Life of Napoleon*, Vol. 2, he writes on page 30:

> "The demand of the Communauté de Paris[5], now the Sanhedrin of the Jacobins, was, of course, for blood."

Again, on page 56 he writes:

> "The power of the Jacobins was irresistible in Paris, where Robespierre, Danton and Marat shared the high places in the synagogue."

Writing of the Commune, Sir Walter Scott states in the same work:

> "The principal leaders of the Commune seem to have been foreigners."

Some of the names of these "foreigners" are worthy of note:

There was Choderlos de Laclos, manager of the Palais Royal, said to be of Spanish origin.

There was Manuel, the Procurer of the Commune, already mentioned. He it was who started the attack upon royalty in the Convention, which culminated with the execution of Louis and Marie Antoinette.

There was David the painter, a leading member of the Committee of Public Security, which "tried" the victims. His voice was always raised calling for death. Sir Walter Scott writes that this fiend used to preface his "bloody work of the day with the professional phrase, 'let us grind enough of the Red'." David it was who inaugurated the

---

[5] [The Paris County Council, equivalent to the L.C.C. in London.]

Cult of the Supreme Being; and organized

> "The conducting of this heathen mummery, which was substituted for every external sign of rational devotion." (Sir Walter Scott, *Life of Napoleon*, Vol. 2.)

There were Reubel and Gohir, two of the five "Directors", who with a Council of Elders became the government after the fall of Robespierre, being known as the Directoire.

The terms "Directors" and "Elders" are, of course, characteristically Jewish.

One other observation should be made here; it is that this important work by Sir Walter Scott in 9 volumes, revealing so much of the real truth, is practically unknown, is never reprinted with his other works, and is almost unobtainable.

Those familiar with Jewish technique will appreciate the full significance of this fact; and the added importance it lends to Sir Walter Scott's evidence regarding the powers behind the French Revolution.

To return to the scene in Paris. Robespierre now remains alone, and apparently master of the scenes; but this again was only appearance. Let us turn to the *Life of Robespierre*, by one G. Renier, who writes as though Jewish secrets were at his disposal. He writes:

> "From April to July 1794 (the fall of Robespierre) the terror was at its height. It was never the dictatorship of a single man, least of all Robespierre. Some 20 men (the Committees of Public Safety and of General

Security) shared the power."

To quote Mr. Renier again:

> "On the 28th July, 1794," "Robespierre made a long speech before the Convention a philippic against ultra-terrorists uttering vague general accusations: 'I dare not name them at this moment and in this place. I cannot bring myself entirely to tear asunder the veil that covers this profound mystery of iniquity. But I can affirm most positively that among the authors of this plot are the agents of that system of corruption and extravagance, the most powerful of all the means invented by foreigners for the undoing of the Republic; I mean the impure apostles of atheism, and the immorality that is at its base'."

Mr Renier continues with all a Jew's satisfaction:

> "Had he not spoken these words he might still have triumphed!"

In this smug sentence Mr Renier unwittingly dots the i's and crosses the t's, which Robespierre had left uncompleted. Robespierre's allusion to the "corrupting and secret foreigners" was getting altogether too near the mark; a little more and the full truth would be out.

At 2 a.m. that night Robespierre was shot in the jaw[6] and

---

[6] In a somewhat similar manner Abraham Lincoln was shot and killed by the Jew Booth on the evening of his pronouncement to his cabinet that he intended in future to finance U.S. loans on a debt free basis similar to the debt free money known as "Greenbacks", with which he had financed the Civil War.

early on the following day dragged to the guillotine.

Again let us recall *Protocol 15*:

> *"In this way we shall proceed with goy masons who know too much."*

THE RUSSIAN REVOLUTION

Monsieur Francois Coty, the celebrated scent manufacturer, wrote in Figaro on 20th February, 1932:

> "The subsidies granted to the Nihilists at this period (1905-1917) by Jacob Schiff, of Kuhn Loeb and Co., New York, were no longer acts of isolated generosity. A veritable Russian terrorist organization had been set up at his expense. It covered Russia with its emissaries."

This creation of terrorist formations by Jews within a country marked down for revolution, whether they be called Nihilists or as in France in 1789, "Sacred Bands", or "Marseillais"; or "Operatives", as in the Britain of Charles I, now stands revealed as standard technique.

Jacob Schiff also financed Japan in her war against Russia 1904-5, as we learn from the Jewish Encyclopaedia.

This war was immediately followed by an attempt at revolution on a considerable scale in Russia, which, however, proved abortive. The next attempt, during the Great War, met with complete success.

On the 3rd January, 1906, the Russian Foreign Minister

supplied to Emperor Nicholas II a report on this revolutionary outbreak, which, as revealed in the American Hebrew of July 13th, 1918, contained the following passages:

> "The events which took place in Russia in 1905 plainly indicate that the revolutionary movement has a definite international character the revolutionaries possess great quantities of arms imported from abroad and very considerable financial means one is bound to conclude that there are foreign capitalists' organizations interested in supporting our revolutionary movement. If we add to the above that, as has been proved beyond any doubt, a very considerable part is played by Jews **as ring-leaders in other organizations** as well as their own... always the most bellicose element of the revolution... we may feel entitled to assume that the above-mentioned foreign support of the Russian revolutionary movement comes from Jewish capitalist circles."

The assumption in the foregoing report was indeed well justified. It was to be confirmed by an even more important official document penned at the height of the revolution itself, in 1918, by Mr. Oudendyke, the representative of the Netherlands Government in St. Petersburg, who was in charge of British interests in Russia after the liquidation of our Embassy by the Bolsheviks.

So important indeed was this report of Mr. Oudendyke's held to be by Mr. Balfour, to whom it was addressed, that it was set out in a British government white paper on bolshevism issued in April 1919. (Russia No. 1.)

In it I have read the following passage:

> "I consider that the immediate suppression of bolshevism is the greatest issue now before the world, not even excluding the war which is still raging, and unless bolshevism is nipped in the bud immediately it is bound to spread in one form or another over Europe, and the whole world, as it is organized and worked by Jews, who have no nationality, and whose one object is to destroy for their own ends the existing order of things."

A still clearer light is thrown on these happenings by an article written on 12th April, 1919, in a paper called *The Communist*, at Kharkov, by one M. Cohen:

> "The great Russian revolution was indeed accomplished by the hands of Jews. There are no Jews in the ranks of the Red Army as far as privates are concerned, but in the Committees, and in the Soviet organization as Commissars, the Jews are gallantly leading the masses. The symbol of Jewry has become the symbol of the Russian proletariat, which can be seen in the fact of the adoption of the five-pointed star, which in former times was the symbol of Zionism and Jewry."

Mr. Fahey, in his important and authenticated work, *The Rulers of Russia*, is more specific, stating that in 1917 of the 52 persons who took over the direction in Russia, all but Lenin were Jews[7].

So thorough was the mass liquidation of all but hewers of wood and drawers of water in Russia, that this Jewish

---

[7] Mr. Fahey must somehow have missed the fact that Lenin himself WAS a Jew. That would mean then that ALL who took over the direction in Russia were Jews.

grip remained unaltered. Dr. Fahey tells us that in 1935 the Central Executive of the Third international, which ruled Russia "consisted of 59 men, of which 56 were Jews. The other three, including Stalin, were married to Jewesses. Of 17 principal Soviet ambassadors, 4 were Jews." (*Rulers of Russia*, pages 8 and 9.)

The Rev. George Simons, who was Superintendent of the Methodist Episcopal Church in St. Petersburg from 1907 to October 1918, appeared before a Committee of the United States Senate on the 12th February, 1919, and gave them a report of his personal knowledge of the happenings in Russia up to the time he left. Dr. Fahey quotes him as saying during this evidence:

> "In December, 1918, out of 388 members of the revolutionary government, only 16 happened to be real Russians; all the rest were Jews with the exception of one U.S. Negro. Two hundred and sixty-five of the Jews come from the Lower East Side of New York."

Such has been the condition of affairs in the U.S.S.R. from that day to this.

Though a number of Jews were liquidated in the so-called "Moscow Purge", this affected the situation in no way. It merely signified that one Jewish faction had triumphed over, and liquidated, another. There has never been anything in the nature of a Gentile revolt against the Jewish domination.

The fact that some Jews were liquidated by winning factions behind the iron curtain could be used to deceive the world outside into thinking that this was the result of an anti-Semitic revolt, and from time to time a hoax of this kind has been systematically propaganded.

As world opinion gradually turned hostile to the U.S.S.R. important Jews began to fear that this feeling, combined with a gradual realization that bolshevism is Jewish, might have unpleasant reactions for them.

About 1945, therefore, a further powerful campaign was organized from influential Jewish circles, notably in the U.S.A., to put out the story once again that Russia had turned on the Jews. They evidently failed, however, to advise their lesser brethren of this move; and indignant and informed denials were soon forthcoming.

A journal called Bulletin, the organ of the Glasgow Discussion Group, wrote in June 1945:

> "Such rubbish as is now being spread as to the growth of anti-Semitism in Russia is nothing but malicious lies and pure invention."

On 1st February, 1949, the *Daily Worker* carried an article in which a Mr. Parker gave a few names and figures of Jews in high office in the U.S.S.R., from which he had evidently recently returned, for he wrote:

> "I never heard a breath of criticism over this state of affairs... anti-Semitism would render a Soviet official liable to prosecution in the same way that a private citizen may be brought before the courts for anti-Semitism."

On the 10th November, 1949, the *Daily Worker*, that constant and burning champion of the Jews, printed an article by Mr D. Kartun, entitled "Stamping Out Anti-

Semitism", which shows the complete Jewish control behind the iron curtain when he writes:

> "In Poland and the other people's democracies anti-Semitism in word or deed is most heavily punished."

Between 1945 and 1949 the propaganda to convince Gentiles outside the iron curtain, that within that area anti-Semitism was rampant, and the Jews driven from high office everywhere was energetically pursued. It began to be believed by quite a number of people, who should have known better; so much so, that in the autumn of the latter year I thought it worthwhile to get out a list showing the number of vital positions held by Jews behind the iron curtain. Here is an extract from those lists.

U.S.S.R.

Premier	Stalin	Married to a Jewess
Vice-Premier	Kaganovitch[8]	Jew
Ministry of State Control	Mekhlis	Jew
Military & Naval Construction Ginsburg	Ginsburg	Jew
Minister Cominform Organ	Yudin	Jew
Chief Publicist Abroad for U.S.S.R.	Ilya Eherenburg	Jew

---

[8] "Kagan" or 'Khagan' is the Khazarian word for 'King'. More than 90% of Jews today are not Semitic, nor are their ancestors. They are of the Turko-Mongolian tribe of Khazars, whose Kagan adopted Talmudism around 740 A.D.

Ministry of Building Enterprises Machinery	Yudin	Jew
Foreign Minister	Molotoff	Married to a Jewess

POLAND

Virtual Ruler	Jacob Bergman	Jew
Public Prosecutor	T. Cyprian	Jew
O.C. Youth Movements	Dr. Braniewsky	Jew

HUNGARY

Virtual Ruler	Mathias Rakosi	Jew

ROUMANIA

Virtual Ruler	Anna Pauker	Jewess

(Since removed for "deviationism" but replaced by another Jew.)

YUGOSLAVIA

Virtual Ruler	Moishe Pyjede	Jew

In May 1949, the Daily Worker, which is, of course, consistently and ardently pro-Jewish, printed an article by Mr A. Rothstein praising the U.S.S.R. to the skies; and about the same time another article on similar lines about the paradise behind the iron curtain by Mr Sam

Aronvitch.

On the 10th November the same paper printed an article in which D. Kartun, writing of the "People's Democracies" and the stamping out of anti-Semitism there, wrote:

> "No one could dream of making an anti-semitic speech or writing an anti-semitic article in any of these countries. If they did their jail sentence would be both immediate and lengthy."

In the last few years we have been supplied with further dramatic proof of the vital inter-relation between Jews and the U.S.S.R.

From the Canadian spy trials, which focused the spotlight on atom spying for the U.S.S.R., with the conviction and imprisonment of Frank Rosenberg (alias Rose), the Canadian Jew Communist Member of Parliament, and several Jews, to the conviction and imprisonment of many others of the same gang in Britain and the U.S.A., including Fuchs, Professor Weinbaum, Judith Coplon, Harry Gold, David Greenglass, Julius Rosenberg, Miriam Moskewitz, Abraham Brothanz, and Raymond Boyer, who — though a Gentile by birth — married a Jewess and, I believe, adopted the Jewish creed on that occasion.

Finally, we had the flight to the U.S.S.R. with atom secrets also of the Jew Professor Pontecorvo, who had been working in close association with Fuchs.

No doubt we shall continue to be regaled with plausible stories proving that Russia has gone anti-semitic; but it is not hard to realise that such a Jewish grip backed by the most elaborate spy and liquidation squads known to man, would cause a convulsion which would shake the world before its grip could be broken.

A. M. RAMSAY

DEVELOPMENT OF REVOLUTIONARY TECHNIQUE

Four revolutions in history merit our special attention. The study and comparison of the methods employed therein will reveal on the one hand a basic similarity between them: and on the other an interesting advance in technique, with each succeeding upheaval. It is as if we studied the various stages in the evolution of the modern rifle from the original old "brown Bess."

The revolutions in question are firstly the Cromwellian, secondly the French, thirdly the Russian, and lastly the Spanish revolution of 1936.

All four can be proved to have been the work of international Jewry. The first three succeeded, and secured the murder of the reigning monarch and the liquidation of his supporters.

In each case Jewish finance, and underground intrigue, are clearly traceable; and the earliest measures passed by the revolutionaries have been "emancipation" for the Jews.

Cromwell was financed by various Jews, notably Manasseh Ben Israel and Carvajal "the Great Jew", contractor to his army.

On this occasion Jewish influence remained financial and commercial, while the propaganda weapons and medium were semi-religious, all the Cromwellians being soaked in Old Testament Judaism; some, such as General Harrison, even carried their Judaism to the length of advocating the adoption of the Mosaic Law as the law of England, and the substitution of Saturday as the Sabbath in place of the Christian Sunday.

We are all familiar with the absurd Old Testament passages which the Roundhead rank and file adopted as names, such as Sergeant Obadiah, "Bind their Kings in chains and their nobles in fetters of iron." The Cromwellian revolution was short-lived. The work of destruction had not been sufficiently thorough to frustrate counter-revolution, and restoration of the old regime.

A second revolution, the so-called "Glorious Revolution" of 1689, was necessary. This again was financed by Jews, notably Solomon Medina, Suasso, Moses Machado and others.

By the French revolution of 1789 the technique had been notably improved. Secret societies had been developed throughout France on a grand scale in the preceding years. The plans for the liquidation of the former regime are by this time far more drastic.

The judicial murder of a kindly and well intentioned King and a few nobles is replaced by mass murders in prisons and in private houses of the whole of the nobility, clergy, gentry and bourgeoisie, regardless of sex.

The Cromwellian damage and desecration of a few churches by their temporary use as stables is developed into a general wrecking of Christian churches, or their conversion into public lavatories, brothels, and markets; and the **banning of the practice of the Christian religion** and even the ringing of church bells.

Civil war is not allowed to develop. The army is sidetracked, and kept apart from its King by his seizure at an early stage. So powerful is the unseen control by 1789 that apparently, the dregs of the French population victoriously liquidate all their natural leaders, in itself a most unnatural and suspicious phenomenon.

More suspicious still is the sudden appearance of strong bands of armed hooligans, who march on Paris from Lyons and Marseilles; and are **recorded as being obviously foreigners.**

Here we have the first formations of alien mercenary and criminal elements, forcing revolutions upon a country not their own, which were to have their finished and expanded prototype in the International Brigades, which attempted to force Marxism on Spain 150 years later.

England in the 17th century had not been dismembered and hideously remoulded on alien lines; but all familiar land marks in 18th century France were destroyed. The splendid and historic names and titles of counties, departments and families were scrapped, and France divided into numbered squares occupied merely by "citizens".

Even the months of the calendar were changed. The national flag of France with its lilies and its glories was banned. Instead the French received the Tricolour, badge of murder and rapine. Here, however, the planners made a mistake.

The Tricolour might not be the honoured and famous flag of France. It might be dripping with the blood of massacre, regicide and villainy. It might be stinking with the slime of the Jewish criminals who designed and foisted it upon the French people; but it was proclaimed the national flag, and the national flag it became; and with the national flag came the national army, and a national leader, Napoleon.

It was not long before this great Frenchman ran up against the secret powers, who up till then controlled the armies of France. They had planned to use these armies to revolutionise all European states, one after another; to overthrow all leadership, and establish rule of the mob, apparently, in reality of course their own.

Just in this manner do the Jews today plan to use the Red Army. Such a policy directed by aliens of this type could not long continue once a national army had thrown up a real national leader; their outlook and policy must inevitably be poles apart. It was not long before the First Consul challenged and overthrew these aliens and their puppets.

By the year 1804 Napoleon had come to recognise the Jew and his plans as a menace to France and all that the revolution had swept away he systematically restored. From this time onwards Jewish money financed every coalition against him; and Jews today boast that it was Rothschild rather than Wellington who defeated Napoleon.

Knowing these things, Hitler, on his occupation of Paris, immediately ordered a permanent guard of honour to be mounted over Napoleon's tomb at the Invalides; and had the body of L'Aiglon (Napoleon's son by Maria Louisa) brought from Austria, and buried at last in his proper place at the side of his father.

When we come to examine the Russian revolution we find that the technique is still bolder and far more drastic. On this occasion no national flag, army, or anthem is permitted. After the dregs of the community have apparently accomplished the impossible, and liquidated every other class down to and including the kulak (a man with three cows), they are herded into a polyglot force called the Red Army; over them waves an international red flag, not a Russian flag; their anthem is the Internationale.

The technique of revolution in Russia was so perfected that to this day it has secured the Jewish regime established there against all counter strokes.

The next revolution to merit our attention is the one that broke out in Spain in 1936. Fortunately for Europe, it was frustrated by General Franco and a number of gallant men, who instantly took the field in opposition to the revolutionary forces, and succeeded in a long struggle in crushing them.

This achievement is all the more remarkable in view of the latest development in revolutionary organisation, which was then revealed in the shape of the International Brigades. These International Brigades, besides representing the very latest novelty in revolutionary technique, were a remarkable production.

They were recruited from criminals, adventurers and dupes, mostly communists, from 52 different countries, mysteriously transported and assembled in formations in Spain within a few weeks of the outbreak of disorder, uniformed in a garb closely related to our battle dress, and armed with weapons bearing the Jewish five-pointed star.

This star and the Seal of Solomon were upon the signet rings of N.C.O.s and Officers in this communist horde of ill-disciplined ruffians. I have seen them myself in wear.

By October 1936 these International Brigades were already assembled in Spain in considerable numbers. Undisciplined and blackguardly though they were, the mere fact of a large and well-armed political army, intervening suddenly on one side in the early stages of a civil war, might reasonably have been counted upon to achieve a decision before the patriotic and decent element in the country could have time to create an adequate fighting machine.

Though the British public were kept in total ignorance as to the true significance of what was taking place in Spain two countries in Europe were alive to the situation. Germany and Italy had each in their turn experienced the throes of communist revolution, and emerged victorious over this foulest of earthly plagues. They knew who had financed and organised the International Brigades; and with what fell purpose Barcelona had been declared in October 1936 the Capital of the Soviet States of Western Europe.

At the critical moment they [Hitler and Mussolini] intervened in just sufficient strength to counter the

International Brigade, and enable the Spanish people to organise their own army, which, in due course, easily settled the matter. Settled the matter, that is to say, as far as Spain was concerned.

There was, however, another settlement to come. International Jewry had been seriously thwarted. They would not rest henceforward until they could have their revenge; until they could by hook or crook turn the guns of the rest of the world against these two States, which in addition to thwarting their designs in Spain were in the process of placing Europe upon a system independent of gold and usury, which, if permitted to develop, would break the Jewish power for ever.

A. M. RAMSAY

GERMANY BELLS THE CAT

The urgent alarm sounded in 1918 by Mr. Oudendyke in his letter to Mr. Balfour, denouncing bolshevism as a Jewish plan, which if not checked by the combined action of the European Powers, would engulf Europe and the world, was no exaggeration.

By the end of that year the red flag was being hoisted in most of the great cities of Europe. In Hungary the Jew Bela Kuhn organised and maintained for some time a merciless and bloody tyranny similar to the one in Russia. In Germany, the Jews Leibknecht, Barth, Scheidemann, Rosa Luxemburg, etc., made a desperate bid for power. These and other similar convulsions shook Europe; but each country in its own way just frustrated the onslaughts.

In most countries concerned a few voices were raised in an endeavour to expose the true nature of these evils. Only in one, however, did a political leader and group arise, who grasped to the full the significance of these happenings, and perceived behind the mobs of native hooligans the organisation and driving power of world Jewry.

This leader was Adolf Hitler, and his group the National

Socialist Party of Germany.

Never before in history had any country not only repulsed organised revolution, but discerned Jewry behind it, and faced up to that fact. We need not wonder that the sewers of Jewish vituperation were flooded over these men and their leader; nor should we make the mistake of supposing that Jewry would stick at any lie to deter honest men everywhere from making a thorough investigation of the facts for themselves.

Nevertheless, if any value liberty, and set out to seek truth and defend it, this duty of personal investigation is one which they cannot shirk. To accept unquestioningly the lies and misrepresentations of a Jew-controlled or influenced press, is to spurn truth by sheer idleness, if for no worse reason.

To act on such unverified a basis is to sin against the Light.

In the case of Germany and Hitler the task of research is not difficult. We have it on many authorities that Hitler's book, *Mein Kampf,* stated fully and accurately the author's observations and conclusions concerning all these vital matters.

Quite false pictures have been propagated deliberately about this book, by quoting passages out of their context, distorting meanings, and downright misrepresentation. Having read many of these unscrupulous diatribes, it was with no little surprise that I read this book for myself not so very long ago.

From many conversations I had heard and taken part in,

I now realise that most members of the public were as ignorant as I of the real nature of this remarkable book. I propose, therefore, to try and give a true picture of its spirit and purport by quotations from its two main themes: Firstly realisation and exposure of the Jewish scheme for world Marxism; and secondly, admiration of, and longing for friendship with Great Britain. Writing of the days before 1914, Hitler states:

> "I still saw Jewry as a religion ... Of the existence of deliberate Jewish hostility I had no conception... I gradually realised that the Social Democratic Press was preponderantly controlled by Jews... There was not a single paper with which Jews were connected which could be described as genuinely national ... I seized all the Social Democratic pamphlets I could get hold of, and looked up the names of their authors - nothing but Jews."

As he pursued the study of these questions, Hitler began to perceive the main outlines of the truth:

> "I made also a deep study of the relation between Judaism and Marxism... The Jewish State never had boundaries as far as space was concerned; it was unlimited as regards space, but bound down by its conception of itself as a race. That people, therefore, was always a State within a State... The Jewish doctrine of Marxism rejects the aristocratic principle in nature... denies the value of the individual among men, combats the importance of nationality and race, thereby depriving humanity of the whole meaning of existence."

> "Democracy in the west today is the forerunner of Marxism, which would be inconceivable without Democracy."

> "If the Jew, with the help of his Marxian creed, conquers the nations of the world, his crown will be the funeral wreath of the human race..."

He writes of the days of 1918:

> "Thus did I now believe that by defending myself against the Jews I am doing the Lord's work."

At the end of 1918 there came the revolution in Germany organised behind the unbroken army in the field. Concerning this Hitler wrote:

> "In November sailors arrived in lorries, and called on us all to revolt, a few Jewish youths being the leaders in that struggle for the 'freedom, beauty and dignity of our national life'. Not one of them had ever been to the Front."

> "The real organiser of the revolution and its actual wire-puller the International Jew... The revolution was not made by the forces of peace and order; but by those of riot, robbery and plunder."

> "I was beginning to learn afresh, and only now (1919) came to a right comprehension of the teachings and intentions of the Jew Karl Marx. Only now did I properly understand his 'Kapital'; and equally also the struggle of Social Democracy against the economics of the nation; and that its aim is to prepare the ground for the domination of the truly international Kapital." [sic] Emperor to offer the hand of friendship to the leaders of Marxism... While they held the Imperial hand in theirs the other hand was already feeling for the dagger."

> "With the Jew there is no bargaining; there is merely

the hard 'either, or'." Later on Hitler gives in great detail the outlines of the Jewish disruptive machine.

"By means of the Trades Unions which might have been the saving of the nation, the Jew actually destroys the nation's economics."

"By creating a press which is on the intellectual level of the least educated, the political and labour organisation obtains force of compulsion enabling it to make the lowest strata of the nation ready for the most hazardous enterprises."

"The Jewish press... tears down all which may be regarded as the prop of a nation's independence, civilisation and its economic autonomy. It roars especially against characters who refuse to bow the knee to Jewish domination, or whose intellectual capacity appears to the Jew in the light of a menace to himself."

"The ignorance displayed by the mass... and the lack of instinctive perception of our upper class make the people easy dupes of this campaign of Jewish lies."

"But the present day is working its own ruin; it introduces universal suffrage, chatters about equal rights, and can give no reason for so thinking. In its eyes material rewards are the expression of a man's worth, thus shattering the basis for the noblest equality that could possibly exist."

"It is one of the tasks of our Movement to hold out prospects of a time when the individual will be given what he needs in order to live; but also to maintain the principle that man does not live for material enjoyment alone."

> "The political life of today alone has persistently turned its back on this principle of nature" (i.e. quality) ..."

> "Human civilisation is but the outcome of the creative force of personality in the community as a whole, and especially among its leaders... the principle of the dignity of the majority is beginning to poison all life below it; and in fact to break it up."

> "We now see that Marxism is the enunciated form of the Jewish attempt to abolish the importance of personality in all departments of human life; and to set up the mass of numbers in its place..."

> "The principle of decision by majorities has not always governed the human race; on the contrary, it only appears during quite short periods of history, and those are always periods of decadence in nations and States."

> "We must not forget that the international Jew, who continues to dominate over Russia, does not regard Germany as an ally, but as a State destined to undergo a similar fate."

On the last page and in almost the last paragraph of Mein Kampf is the following:

> "The party as such stands for positive Christianity, but does not bind itself in the matter of creed to any particular confession. It combats the Jewish materialistic spirit within us and without us."

Looking round the world for help in the battle against this terrible menace of Jew directed bolshevism, Hitler's mind constantly reverted to Britain and the British Empire. He always longed for their friendship. Always declared Britain to be one of the greatest bulwarks against chaos; and that her interests and those of Germany were complementary and not contrary to one another.

He wrote:

> "It was not a British interest but in the first place a Jewish one to destroy Germany." And again: "Even in England there is a continual struggle going on between the representatives of British state interests and the Jewish world dictatorship."
>
> "Whilst England is exhausting herself in maintaining her position in the world, the Jew is organising his measures for its conquest... Thus the Jew today is a rebel in England, and the struggle against the Jewish world menace will be started there also."
>
> "No sacrifice would have been too great in order to gain England's alliance. It would have meant renunciation of the colonies and importance at sea, and refraining from interference with British industry by competition."

In later years these two themes were ceaselessly expounded; viz., the Jewish Marxist menace, and the eagerness for friendship with Britain. Even down to, and including Dunkirk, Hitler pressed the latter idea on all and sundry; even on his highest Generals, to their astonishment.

Nor did he stop at words, as will be shown later when, as Liddell Hart informs us, he saved the British Army from annihilation by halting the Panzer Corps, informing his Generals the while, that he regarded the British Empire and the Catholic Church as necessary bulwarks of peace and order which must be safeguarded.[9]

Before it had left the printers, the floodgates of Jewish hatred and lies had been full- opened against Hitler and the Third Reich all over the world.

English-speaking people everywhere were deluged with fabrications, distortions and atrocity stories, which drowned the voices of the few who understood the real situation.

Forgotten in the turmoil was Marx's slogan that before bolshevism could triumph the British Empire must be destroyed; and totally suppressed as far as the British people were concerned was Hitler's repeated declaration of his willingness to defend the British Empire if called upon to assist by force of arms if necessary.

---

[9] *The Other Side of the Hill*, Chap. X, by Liddell Hart. Mein Kampf was first published in October 1933.

1933: JEWRY DECLARES WAR

The English edition of *Mein Kampf* was still in the process of printing and publication when Jewry declared war on the national Socialist regime, and started an intensive blockade against Germany.

The International Jewish Boycott Conference was assembled in Holland in the summer of 1933 under the Presidency of Mr. Samuel Untermeyer, of the U.S.A., who was elected President of the World Jewish Economic Federation formed to combat the opposition to Jews in Germany.

On his return to the U.S.A., Mr Untermeyer gave an address over Station W.A.B.C., the text of which, as printed in the *New York Times* of August 7th, 1933, I have before me. Mr Untermeyer referred in the opening phrases to:

> "The holy war in the cause of humanity in which we are embarked"; and proceeded to develop the subject at great length, describing the Jews as the aristocrats of the world. "Each of you, Jew and Gentile alike, who has not already enlisted in this sacred war[10] should do so

---

[10] Like the never ending war on "terror" today

now and here."

Those Jews who did not join in he denounced, declaring:

"They are traitors to their race."

In January 1934 Mr. Jabotinsky, founder of Revisionist Zionism, wrote in *Natcha Retch*:

"The fight against Germany has been carried out for months by every Jewish community, conference, trade organisation, by every Jew in the world... we shall let loose a spiritual and a material war of the whole world against Germany."

This is perhaps the most confident assertion extant on the Jewish claim, set out in the *Protocols of Zion*, that they can bring about war. *Protocol Number 7* states:

"We must be in a position to respond to every act of opposition by a State by war with its neighbour. If these should venture to stand collectively, by universal war."

It should be remembered here that a copy of these Protocols was filed in the British Museum in 1906.

By 1938 the Jewish war was in full swing; and already through their influence or pressure many Gentile persons and groups were being drawn into the vortex. Various members of the British Socialist Party were openly advocating joining in this cold war; and a vigorous and uncompromising clique was growing in all Parties under the leadership of Messrs' Churchill, Amery, Duff, Cooper and others.

"Hitler will have no war, but he will be forced to it, not this year, but later on," screamed the Jew Emil Ludwig in the June copy of *Les Aniles* 1934.

On June 3rd, 1938, matters were carried a long step further by an article in the *American Hebrew*, the weekly organ of American Jewry. This article, which opened by showing that Hitler never deviated from his Mein Kampf doctrine, went on to threaten the direst retaliation.

> "It has become patent that a combination of Britain, France and Russia will sooner or later bar the triumphant march (of Hitler)...
>
> Either by accident or design, a Jew has come to a position of foremost importance in each of these nations. In the hands of non-Aryans lies the fate and the very lives of millions...
>
> In France the Jew of prominence is Leon Blum... Leon Blum may yet be the Moses who will lead...
>
> Maxim Litvinoff, Soviet super salesman, is the Jew who sits at the right hand of Stalin, the little tin soldier of communism...
>
> The English Jew of prominence is Leslie Hore-Belisha, Tommy Atkins' new boss."

Later in this article we read:

> "So it may come to pass that these three sons of Israel will form the combine that will send the frenzied Nazi dictator to hell. And when the smoke of battle clears ... and the man who played the swastikaed Christus... is lowered into a hole in the ground... as the trio of non-

> Aryans intone a ramified requiem... a medley of the marseillaise, God Save the King, and the Internationale, blending with a proud and aggressive rendering of Eli Eli."

Two points in the above extract are worthy of special note. Firstly, it is taken for granted that these three Jews will not for one moment think or act as anything but Jews; and can be relied upon to guide their Gentile dupes to ruin in a plainly Jewish war; secondly, should be noted the contemptuous reference to the "swastikaed Christus," which Jewry looks forward to burying; and which reveals by its classification the Jewish hatred of Christianity.

Meantime Jewish pressure was exerted to the utmost to incite clashes between Sudeten, Czechs, Poles and Germans.

By September of 1938 matters had reached a desperate pass. Mr. Chamberlain himself flew out to Munich and achieved the historic settlement with Hitler. It seemed as though the war mongers had been frustrated, and Europe saved. Rarely had such scenes and evidences of spontaneous delight and thankfulness been evoked as were witnessed throughout Britain and Europe at that triumph.

Those who knew the power of the enemy, however, knew that Mr Chamberlain's work was certain to be swiftly sabotaged. I remember remarking, on the very evening of his return from Munich, that within a week every newspaper in this country and the war mongers in Parliament, would be attacking Mr Chamberlain for having secured peace; regardless of the fact that in so doing they were contemptuously flouting the real wishes of the people. This remark was only too true, as events proved.

Nowhere was the Jewish fury so obvious, of course, as in Moscow. I have before me a leaflet of my own designing put out in October 1938. It runs:

> "Are you aware that Mr. Chamberlain was burnt in effigy in Moscow as soon as it was known that he had secured peace; showing very clearly Who Wanted War, and who are still ceaselessly working to stir up strife all the world over."

The attempt to provoke war over Sudetenland and Czechoslovakia having failed, there remained only the detonator in the Polish Corridor, that monstrosity born of the unholy Versailles Conference, and denounced by honest men from Marshal Foch and Arthur Henderson, from that time onwards.

One feature about the Versailles Conference has been kept secret by those who possess the power to keep things from the public or to proclaim things from the house tops. It is this:

All important decisions were taken by the "Big Four" - Britain, France, Italy and the U.S.A., represented respectively by Mr. Lloyd George, M. Clemenceau, Baron Sonino and President Wilson. So much is known. What is not known is that:

The secretary of Mr. Lloyd George was the Jew Sassoon; of M. Clemenceau the Jew Mandel Rothschild, now known as Mandel;

Baron Sonino was himself half a Jew: and President Wilson had the Jew Brandeis;

The interpreter was another Jew named Mantoux; and the Military Adviser yet another Jew called Kish.

It is known that Mr Lloyd George and others were hazy about geography. Their Jewish secretaries, however, were on the contrary very much on the spot on such matters. These Jews met at 6 p.m. in the evenings; and mapped out the decisions for the following day's conference of the "Big Four."

The results were disastrous from the point of view of all decent people, who hoped for an honourable treaty, with terms which, though they might be stringent, would at least be just and thereby secure lasting peace.

Foch himself loudly denounced the treaty; declaring that it contained the certain makings of another war and deprecating in particular the provision relating to Danzig and the Corridor.

Arthur Henderson and many public men joined in the denunciation; but all to no avail. From the point of view of men planning another war, however, nothing could have been better than this treaty.

All sorts of glaring injustices were ingrained in its text. In addition to the Corridor, and the position at Danzig, a bastard State was brought into being, in which Germans, Slovaks, etc., together forming a majority of the country, were put under the tyrannical control of the Czech minority, an element which had thrown in its lot with the Bolshevik Jews and fought against the Allies in 1918.

The design of this State was such geographically that it was styled, and correctly styled, a dagger pointed at the heart of Germany. It received the outlandish name of Czechoslovakia.

The whole of the industrial life from the huge Skoda arsenal downwards was controlled by Jewish banking interests; while we have it on the evidence of Lord Winterton that practically all the land was mortgaged to the Jews (Hansard, October 1936).

Under this Messianic domination were enslaved huge sections of populations, belonging to other nations, henceforward condemned to be held down by force until some country should grow strong enough to champion them.

This eventuality was, in my opinion, visualised and actually fostered as we know by the huge loans to Germany from international banking interests.

Let it not be forgotten that while Jewish bankers were pouring money into Germany which was rebuilding the Wehrmacht on a bigger scale than ever, a colossal campaign for peace and disarmament was launched in this country. This not only succeeded in substantially disarming us; but in creating an atmosphere in which Mr Baldwin had to admit that he dared not go to the country asking for more armaments, vital though he knew our needs in sea, air and land forces to be.[11]

To anyone who made a study of the personalities and

---

[11] All prior of course to the rise of Hitler.

powers behind this so-called peace propaganda, as I did, there can be no doubt as to whence the real drive and finance emanated.

To anyone appreciating the attitude of the press at that time, and realising that had this disarmament propaganda been distasteful to those who influence our publicity services, there would have blared forth a torrent of invective against our "peace ballotters"; there is additional proof that this campaign had the support of international Jewry, as had the rearmament of Germany. But why? The simple will ask.

The answer is fairly simple, if once the purpose behind the Jewish plan is understood.

> "Out of the last war we brought the Soviet States of Russia; out of the next war we will bring the Soviet States of Europe..."

had been the pronouncement at a world meeting of communist parties about 1932. To make the next war possible, therefore, the see-saw must be balanced again; German strength built up, and British strength whittled down.

Then the Europeans can fight each other to the death of one and complete exhaustion of the other.

A dramatic surprise is in store for both sides. Neither is to be the real winner. The real winner is quite a different army. This army is the one that will receive the real attention. For 25 years it will be built up under conditions of the greatest secrecy. Its leaders will not show their strength until the conflict is well under way.

Not until a critical moment in the war will the European armies be permitted to guess at the existence of the huge factories [12] beyond the Urals, or of the colossal proportions of the heavily mechanised hordes which will then commence to roll westwards over Europe under the red flag of Marxism.

In March 1939 a British guarantee to Poland was given by Mr. Chamberlain on the strength of a false report to the effect that a 48-hour ultimatum had been delivered by Germany to the Poles.

This report subsequently turned out to be quite untrue. The guarantee had been given, however, and the decision of peace or war was now no longer in British hands. Jewry had the ball at its feet. Can we doubt but that Poland was encouraged to ignore the German note of March which set forth eminently reasonable suggestions for a peaceful solution of the problem of the Corridor?

Month after month no reply was vouchsafed by Poland to the German note. Meanwhile, insult and outrage occurred with suspicious frequency all along the German frontier, similar to the technique to which the Jews later introduced the British in Palestine.

Day after day the British public was deluged with war propaganda and misrepresentation of the situation. Finally their minds were closed against any further

---

[12] These "huge factories" and "colossal proportions of the heavily mechanised hords" are thanks to the American people, via the Lend Lease Act, implemented before Americans were sucked into that war, and minutely detailed in the Diaries of Major Jordan (George Racey Jordan).

regard to the demands of justice or reason by a new slogan,

> "You cannot trust Hitler's word."

With this lie the British public was finally stampeded into throwing all reason and judgment to the winds and accepting at their face value the war propaganda in the press.

This slogan was founded upon a misrepresentation of Hitler's assurance given on more than one occasion after a "putsch" such as that into Sudetenland, that he "intended to make no further demands."

The misrepresentation lay in the fact that the press steadily obscured the major fact, that the "demands" to which Hitler referred were all along five fold in character; and covered those five areas taken from Germany by a dictated peace in which the population was overwhelmingly German, i.e. Sudetenland, part of Czechoslovakia, parts of Poland, the Corridor and Danzig.

As German troops occupied each successive section, it is, I believe, accurate to say that Hitler declared, that he had no additional demands to make. But here it must be clearly stated in the interests of justice that he never said that this entailed reducing the demands which he had originally very clearly delineated, and repeated on many occasions, namely, the five areas in question.

The British public was deluded by its press into supposing that when Hitler said he had no further demands, that there had never been any statement of his full demands, some of which were still unfulfilled. They were led to believe that Hitler either never had any other demands, or that he had abandoned the rest as soon as he had obtained some of them.

When, therefore, the next instalment was added, the press built on this misunderstanding the fallacy that Hitler's word could not be trusted. Honest dealing needs no such trickery and deception. Such methods are only necessary to bolster up bad or unjust causes.

Fortunately we have the calm and dispassionate judgment in this matter by no less a person than the late Lord Lothian, recently British Ambassador to the U.S.A. In his last speech at Chatham House on this subject he remarked:

"If the principle of self-determination had been applied in Germany's favour, as it was applied against her, it would have meant the return of Sudetenland, Czechoslovakia, parts of Poland, the Polish Corridor, and Danzig to the Reich." Here is a very different presentment of the case to the one which was foisted upon the British public in 1939; and it is the true one. Small wonder that these facts had to be withheld from the ordinary citizen.

Had the British public realised the truth, that each of these demands of Hitler's rested on a foundation of reasonable fairness, the people of this island would have ruled out any question of war; and it was war, not truth or justice, upon which international Jewry was resolved.

"PHONEY WAR" ENDED BY CIVILIAN BOMBING

Though a state of war was declared to exist between Britain and Germany in September of 1939, it very soon became apparent that no war was being conducted by Germany against this country.

This was no surprise to those who knew the facts of the case. Hitler had again and again made it clear, that he never intended to attack or harm Great Britain or the British Empire. With the Siegfried Line strongly held, and no German intention of appearing west of it, stalemate in the west, or the "Phoney War," as it came to be called, must, in the absence of bombing of civilian populations ultimately peter out altogether.

No one was quicker to perceive this than the pro-Jewish war mongers; and they and their friends inside and outside the House of Commons very soon began exerting pressure for this form of bombing of Germany to be started.

On 14th January, 1940, *The Sunday Times* gave prominence to a letter from an anonymous correspondent, who demanded to know why we were not using our air power "to increase the effect of the blockade."

"Scrutator," in the same issue, commented on this letter as follows:

> "Such an extension of the offensive would inevitably develop into competitive frightfulness. It might be forced on us in reprisals for enemy action, and we must be in a position to make reprisals if necessary. But the bombing of industrial towns, with its unavoidable loss of life among the civilian population -- that is what it would come to -- would be inconsistent with the spirit, if not the actual words of the pledges given from both sides at the beginning of the war."

The above quotation is taken from a book entitled *Bombing Vindicated*, which was published in 1944 by Mr. J. M. Spaight, C.B., C.B.E., who was the principal assistant secretary at the Air Ministry during the war. As its title suggests, this book is an attempt to justify the indiscriminate use of bombers against the civil population. In it Mr. Spaight boasts that this form of bombing "saved civilisation": and reveals the startling fact that **it was Britain that started this ruthless form of war on the very evening of the day on which Mr. Churchill became Prime Minister, May 11th, 1940.**

On page 64 of his book, Mr. Spaight gives a further piece of information, which renders this sudden change of British policy all the more astonishing; for he states that a declaration was made by the British and French Governments on 2nd September, 1939, that

> "Only strictly military objectives in the narrowest sense of the word would be bombarded."

This declaration, of course, was made in the days of Mr Chamberlain's Premiership; and no single fact perhaps could demarcate and differentiate more clearly the difference in the character and behaviour between Mr. Chamberlain and Mr. Churchill.

On the 27th January, 1940, thirteen days after the letter in *The Sunday Times* already quoted, *The Daily Mail* endorsed editorially the views which had been expressed in that issue by "Scrutator"; and it devoted a leading article, writes Mr. Spaight, to combating the suggestion of Mr. Amery and others that we should start the bombing of Germany.

Sir Duff Cooper had written on the previous day in the same paper that

> "There would appear to exist a kind of unwritten truce between the two belligerents, according to the tacit terms of which they do not bomb one another."

In view of the declaration by Britain and France of September 2nd, 1939, that they would "only bomb military objectives in the narrowest sense of the word," Sir Duff Cooper's verbiage about "a kind of unwritten truce," seems to me gravely obscurantist, if honest.

Inside the House of Commons, the pro-Jewish war mongers were now becoming more and more intransigent; and more and more set on sabotaging the chances of turning the "phoney war" into a negotiated peace. This in spite of the fact that Britain had nothing to gain by further and total war, and everything to lose.

The Jews, of course, had everything to lose by a peace which left the German gold- free money system and Jew-free Government intact, and nothing to gain.

It seemed clearer to me every day that this struggle over the question of civilian bombing was the crux of the whole matter; and that by this method of warfare alone could the Jews and their allies cut the Gordian knot of stalemate leading to peace; and probably later on to a joint attack on Jewish Bolshevism in Russia.

Accordingly, on 15th February 1940, I put down the following question to the Prime Minister: Captain Ramsay asked the Prime Minister:

> "Whether he will assure the House that H.M. Government will not assent to the suggestions made to them, to abandon those principles which led them to denounce the bombing of civilian populations in Spain and elsewhere, and embark upon such a policy themselves?"

Mr Chamberlain himself replied in outspoken terms:

> "I am unaware of the suggestions to which my honourable and gallant friend refers. The policy of H.M. Government in this matter was fully stated by myself in answer to a question by the honourable Member for Bishop Auckland (Mr Dalton) on 14th September last.
>
> In the course of that answer I said that whatever be the length to which others may go, H.M. Government will never resort to the deliberate attack on women and children, and other civilians, for purposes of mere terrorism. I have nothing to add to that answer."

Both this question and the reply were evidently distasteful in the extreme to the war mongers, so I resolved to carry the matter a stage further. On 21st

February I put down another question on the subject: Captain Ramsay asked the Prime Minister:

> "Whether he is aware that the Soviet aeroplanes are carrying on a campaign of bombing civil populations, and whether H.M. Government have dispatched protests on the subject similar to those dispatched during the Civil War in Spain in similar circumstances?"

Mr. Butler replied for the Prime Minister:

> "Yes, Sir. The Soviet Air Forces have pursued a policy of indiscriminate bombing, which cannot be too strongly condemned. H.M. Government have not, however, lodged any protest, since there are unfortunately no grounds for supposing that such action would achieve the result desired."

There can be little doubt but that these two downright answers crystallised the resolves of the war mongers to get rid of a Prime Minister whose adherence to an upright and humane policy must inevitably frustrate their plans, seeing that **Hitler wished no war with Britain, and would therefore never start civilian bombing himself**.

The machinery of intrigue and rebellion against Mr. Chamberlain was set in motion. Ultimately he was saddled with the blame for the Norway blunder; and this pretext was used by the Churchillian-cum-Socialist caucus to secure his downfall.

It should be remembered in this connection that prior to and during the Norway gamble, **Mr Churchill had been invested with full powers and responsibilities for all Naval Military and Air operations; and if anyone**

therefore deserved to be broken over that second Gallipoli (pursued in defiance of high naval authority warning that, without control of the Cattegat and Skaggerack it could not possibly succeed) **it should have been the Minister responsible.**

He however was not only unbroken, he was acclaimed Prime Minister. The man who would tear up the British pledge of September 2nd, 1939, and start bombing the civilians of Germany was the man for the war mongers who now ruled the roost.

And so civilian bombing [by England] **started on the evening that the architect of the Norwegian fiasco became Prime Minister, viz., May 11th, 1940.**

DUNKIRK AND AFTER

Captain Liddell Hart, the eminent military critic, wrote a book on the military events of 1939-45, which was published in 1948, and entitled *The Other Side of the Hill*.

Chapter 10 - which deals with the German invasion of France down to and including Dunkirk - bears the somewhat startling title, "How Hitler beat France and saved Britain."

The reading of the chapter itself will astound all propaganda-blinded people, even more than the title: for the author therein proves that not only did Hitler save this country; but that this was not the result of some unforeseen factor, or indecision, or folly, but was of set purpose, based on his long enunciated and faithfully maintained principle.

Having given details of how Hitler peremptorily halted the Panzer Corps on the 22nd May, and kept them inactive for the vital few days, till, in fact, the British troops had got away from Dunkirk, Captain Liddell Hart quotes Hitler's telegram to Von Kleist:

> "The armoured divisions are to remain at medium artillery range from Dunkirk. Permission is only granted for reconnaissance and protective movements."

Von Kleist decided to ignore the order, the author tells us. To quote him again:

> "Then came a more emphatic order, that I was to withdraw behind the canal. My tanks were kept halted there for three days."

In the following words the author reports a conversation which took place on May 24th (i.e. two days later) between Herr Hitler and Marshal Von Runstedt, and two key men of his staff:

> "He then astonished us by speaking with admiration of the British Empire, of the necessity for its existence, and of the civilisation that Britain had brought into the world...
>
> He compared the British Empire with the Catholic Church - saying they were both essential elements of stability in the world. He said that all he wanted from Britain was that she should acknowledge Germany's position on the continent.
>
> The return of Germany's lost colonies would be desirable, but not essential, and he would even offer to support Britain with troops, if she should be involved in any difficulties anywhere.
>
> He concluded by saying that his aim was to make peace with Britain, on a basis that she would regard compatible with her honour to accept."

Captain Liddell Hart comments on the above as follows:

> "If the British Army had been captured at Dunkirk, the British people might have felt that their honour had suffered a stain, which they must wipe out. By letting it

escape, Hitler hoped to conciliate them. This conviction of Hitler's deeper motive was confirmed by his strangely dilatory attitude over the subsequent plans for the invasion of England."

"He showed little interest in the plans," Blumentritt said, "and made no effort to speed up the preparation. That was utterly different to his usual behaviour. Before the invasion of Poland, of France, and later of Russia, he repeatedly spurred them on; but on this occasion he sat back."

The author continues:

"Since the account of his conversation at Charleville, and subsequent holding back, comes from a section of the Generals, who had long distrusted Hitler's policy, that makes their testimony all the more notable."

And later he goes on to say:

"Significantly their account of Hitler's thoughts about England at the decisive hour before Dunkirk, fits in with much that he himself wrote earlier in Mein Kampf; and it is remarkable how closely he followed his own Bible in other respects."

Anyone who has read Mein Kampf will immediately appreciate the accuracy of the above statement. It is indeed if anything an understatement. Throughout that remarkable book runs two main themes, as I have shown in an earlier chapter - the one, a detailed delineation and denunciation of the Jewish Capitalist-Revolutionary machine; the other, admiration for and eagerness for friendship with Britain and the Empire.

It is a pity, indeed, that so few persons in this island have read this book for themselves; and it is a tragedy that they have instead swallowed wholesale, the unscrupulous distortions and untrue propaganda on the subject, served up to them by Jewish publicity machinery, operating through our press and radio.

Let these people but try and obtain a copy of that book; and when they find they cannot, let them reflect, that if indeed its contents confirmed the lies that they have been told concerning it and its author, the powers behind our publicity would ensure that everyone should be able to secure a copy at the cheapest possible rate.

In any event, I would urge my countrymen to ponder most earnestly the following facts.

The Jew Karl Marx laid it down, that Bolshevism could never really succeed till the British Empire had been utterly destroyed.

Hitler laid it down, that the British Empire was an essential element of stability in the world; and even declared himself ready to defend it with troops, if it should be involved in difficulties anywhere.

By unscrupulous propaganda on an unprecedented scale this country was led into destroying those who wished to be her friends, and offered their lives to defend her; and exalting those, who proclaimed that her destruction was a necessary preliminary to the success of their ideology, forfeiting her Empire and her economic independence in the process.

THE SHAPE OF THINGS TO COME

If the new-found knowledge of Hitler's anxiety to preserve the British Empire has come as a surprise recently to many people in this country, it must surely have come as a real shock to them to learn that **President Roosevelt**, on the other hand, was its inveterate enemy; that he was not only a pro-communist of Jewish origin, but that before he brought America into the war he made it clear that he wished to break up the British Empire.

His son, Colonel Elliot Roosevelt, makes this last point very clear in his book, *As He Saw It*, recently published in the U.S.A.

On pages 19 to 28 of this book, Colonel Roosevelt tells us that in August 1941, his Father, having given out to the American people that he was going off on a fishing trip, actually proceeded to a meeting with Mr. Churchill on board a warship in Argentia Bay.

Lord Beaverbrook, Sir Edward Cadogan, and Lord Cherwell (Professor Lindeman of doubtful race and nationality), and Mr. Averell Harriman were present, he says.

On page 35 he quotes his Father as saying,

> "After the war... there will have to be the greatest possible freedom of trade... no artificial barriers."

Mr. Churchill referred to the British Empire Trade Agreements, and Mr. Roosevelt replied:

> "Yes. Those Empire Trade Agreements are a case in point. It's because of them that the peoples of India, Africa, and of all the Colonial Near East are still as backward as they are...
>
> I can't believe that we can fight a war against Fascist slavery, and at the same time not work to free people all over the world from a backward colonial policy."

"The peace," said Father firmly, "cannot include any continued despotism."

This insolent talk against the British Empire became so pronounced that on page 31 Colonel Roosevelt reports Mr. Churchill as saying,

> "Mr. President, I believe you are trying to do away with the British Empire."

This comment was very near the mark, as the President had been talking about India, Burma, Egypt, Palestine, Indo-China, Indonesia, and all the African Colonies having to be "freed."

On page 115, the Colonel reports his Father as saying:

> "Don't think for a moment, Elliot, that Americans would be dying in the Pacific tonight if it hadn't been for the short-sighted greed of the French, the British and the Dutch. Shall we allow them to do it all over

again?"

These were not at all the reasons, however, given for the war, and for which Americans thought they were dying; nor indeed does the President make any reference as to the pretexts given to his countrymen for the war.

The British, dying in greater numbers, have on the contrary been told that they are dying to defend their Empire from Hitler's wicked plans. Little do they suspect, that it is their so-called ally who plans its destruction.

The President is reported as saying, on page 116:

> "When we've won the war, I will see that the U.S.A. is not wheedled into any plans that will aid or abet the British Empire in its Imperialist ambitions."

And a few pages later:

> "I have tried to make it clear to Winston and the others... that they must never get the idea that we are in it just to help them hang on to the archaic and medieval Empire ideas."

Those who sup with the devil need a long spoon. Mr. Churchill, the self-styled "constant architect of the Jews' future," now found himself playing second fiddle to an even more trusted architect; so eminent, in fact, that he did not make any silly pretensions of respect for the British Empire.

The earlier Moses, Karl Marx, had denounced the Empire long ago, and in the year 1941, it was only foolish opponents of Judaism and Marxism, like Herr Hitler, who were anxious to stand by that Empire, because they recognised it as a bulwark of Christian civilisation.

Although, as we have seen, Mr. Churchill is shown in this book as getting a little petulant from time to time over the President's pronouncements regarding the liquidation of the Empire, this did not prevent him from announcing himself later to the House of Commons as "Roosevelt's ardent lieutenant."

Under what special circumstances the King's Prime Minister could be an ardent lieutenant of a Republican President, whose design it was to destroy that Monarch's Empire, Mr. Churchill did not explain; nor has he yet done so. On another occasion, Mr. Churchill made an equally cryptic remark. He assured the House of Commons,

> "It is no part of my duties, to preside over the liquidation of the British Empire."

No, indeed! Nor was it any part of his duties, on being told that it was to be liquidated, to pronounce himself to be the ardent lieutenant of the would-be liquidator. Nor, we might add, when Minister of Defence, with Admiralty and other codes at his disposal, was it any part of his duties, as Mr Chamberlain's lieutenant, albeit not very ardent, to conduct a personal correspondence of the nature which he did conduct with President Roosevelt by means of the top secret code of the American Foreign Office.

PRESIDENT ROOSEVELT'S ROLE

In my Statement to the Speaker and Members of the House of Commons concerning my detention (see Appendix 1) I summed up at the end of Part 1, the considerations which led me to inspect the secret U.S. Embassy papers at Mr. Tyler Kent's flat in the last weeks of Mr. Chamberlain's Premiership.

The first two of these six considerations were as follows:

Together with many members of both Houses of Parliament, I was fully aware that among the agencies both here and abroad, which had been actively engaged in promoting bad feeling between Great Britain and Germany, organised Jewry, for obvious reasons, had played a leading part.

I knew the U.S.A. to be the headquarters of Jewry, and therefore the real, though not apparent, centre of their activities. It was not until 1948 that corroborative evidence of the foregoing from unimpeachable American sources came into my hands; but when it did come, however, the authentic and fully documented character of the work left nothing to be desired.

I refer to the book by Professor Charles Beard entitled *President Roosevelt and the Coming of the War 1941*, which was published by the Yale University Press in April 1948. This book, which comes with all the authority of its eminent author, is nothing less than a tremendous indictment of President Roosevelt on three main issues.

Firstly, that he got himself elected on the strength of repeated promises, to the effect that he would keep the U.S.A. out of any European war; secondly, that he incessantly and flagrantly disregarded not only his promises to the American people, but all the laws of neutrality; thirdly, that at a predetermined moment he deliberately converted this cold war, which he had been conducting, into a shooting war, by sending the Japanese an ultimatum, which no one could imagine could result in anything but immediate war.

From many instances given relating to the first issue, I quote one:

> "At Boston on October 30th, 1940, he (F.D.R.) was even more emphatic, for there he declared: 'I have said this before, but I shall say it again and again and again: Your boys are not going to be sent into any foreign wars';

And on December 29th:

> 'You can therefore nail any talk about sending armies to Europe as deliberate untruth'."

Professor Beard goes on to prove that while Mr. Roosevelt was making these speeches, he was treating international laws of neutrality with total disregard, and in the interests only of those who were fighting the Jews' battles. The two main forms of non-shooting intervention were the convoying of U.S. ships of ammunition and supplies for the allies, and the Lend Lease Act.

Whatever be our sentiments in appreciating the help of the U.S. arsenals and navy under these two cold war decisions of Mr. Roosevelt, no one can pretend that they were either in accordance with his pledges to the American people, or the fundamentals of international law regarding neutrality.

Some very plain speaking went on in Congress over these acts of the President's. Representative U. Burdick, of North Dakota, said:

> "All our aid to Britain may mean anything... To sell her supplies is one thing... to sell her supplies and convoy them is another thing, to have actual war is the last thing - the last thing is inevitable from the first thing!"

Representative Hugh Paterson, of Georgia, said:

> "It is a measure of aggressive war."

Representative Dewey Short, of Missouri, said:

> "You cannot be half-way in war, and half-way out of war... You can dress this measure up all you please (Lend-Lease), you can sprinkle it with perfume and pour powder on it... but it is still foul and stinks to high heaven."

Representative Philip Bennett, of Missouri, declared:

> "This conclusion is inescapable, that the President is reconciled to active military intervention if such intervention is needed to defeat the Axis in this war.

But our boys are not going to be sent abroad, says the President.

Nonsense, Mr Chairman; even now their berths are being built in our transport ships. Even now the tags for identification of the dead and wounded are being printed by the firm of William C. Ballantyne and Co., of Washington."

Professor Beard proves the third point at great length, showing how at the appropriate moment President Roosevelt forced the Japanese into war by an ultimatum demanding instant compliance with terms, which could never have been accepted by any country. "The memorandum which Senator Hull, with the approval of President Roosevelt, handed to Japan on 26th November, 1941... amounted to the maximum terms of an American policy for the whole Orient." writes Professor Beard, and goes on to say:

> "It required no profound knowledge of Japanese history, institutions, and psychology to warrant... first that no Japanese Cabinet 'liberal or reactionary,' could have accepted the provisions."

And again later:

> "The Japanese agent regarded the American memorandum as a kind of ultimatum. This much at least Secretary Hull knew on November 26th."

Thus was the period of maximum intervention short of a shooting war terminated, and a save-face forged for Roosevelt to ship U.S. boys overseas without apparently breaking the spirit of his many promises.

As the war proceeded the real policy and sympathies of the President became more and more apparent. His deception of the British and their Allies was no less flagrant than his deception of the American people.

As Professor Beard points out on page 576:

> "The noble principles of the Four Freedoms, and the Atlantic Charter were for practical purposes discarded in the settlements, which accompanied the progress and followed the conclusion of the war.
>
> To the validity of this statement the treatment of the people of Esthonia, Lithuania, Poland, Roumania, Yugoslavia, China, Indo-China, Indonesia, Italy, Germany and other places of the earth bear witness."

Some great driving force was clearly at work to induce a President of the United States so to act.

We have seen from a previous chapter that it was not the preservation of the British Empire, nor the French Empire, nor the Dutch, that swayed the President. On the contrary, he had advised his ardent lieutenant, Mr. Churchill, at an early stage in the cold war that these must be liquidated.

It was not Europe, nor the countries of Europe, nor their liberties, nor rights under the Atlantic Charter of Four Freedoms which weighed with him.

We know now that the British and American armies were actually halted by General Ike Eisenhower under Mr. Roosevelt's rulings at the Yalta Conference, so that the Red Army of Jewish Bolshevism might overflow half

Europe and occupy Berlin.

To quote again from Professor Beard:

> "As a consequence of the war called necessary to overthrow Hitler's despotism,' another despotism was raised to a higher pitch of power."

In conclusion, Professor Beard condenses the many indictments of the President set forth in his book, into 12 major counts, and declares:

> "If these precedents are to stand unimpeached, and to provide sanctions for the continued conduct of America affairs - the Constitution may be nullified by the President and officers who have taken the oath and are under moral obligation to uphold it.

For limited Government under supreme law they may substitute personal and arbitrary government -- the first principle of the totalitarian system against which it has been alleged that World War II was waged-while giving lip service to the principle of constitutional government."

When we reflect upon the astounding contents of Professor Beard's book, and consider them in conjunction with the revelations in Colonel Roosevelt's *As He Saw It*, the question arises: whom, and which interests did President Roosevelt not betray.

To this query I can only see one answer, namely, those people and their interests who planned from the start the use of United States arsenals and Forces to prosecute a war which would annihilate a Europe which had **freed itself from Jewish gold** and revolutionary control:

people who planned to dissolve the British Empire, to forge chains of unrepayable debt, wherewith to coerce Britain to this end; and to enable the Soviets to "bestride Europe like a colossus," in other words, International Jewry.[13]

---

[13] These very words were used by General Smuts, who added words to the effect that he welcomed such a prospect. It should be remembered that General Smuts was formerly chief legal adviser to the Zionist Organisation in S. Africa.

A. M. RAMSAY

REGULATION 18B

On the 23rd May, 1940, within the first fortnight of Mr Churchill's Premiership, many hundreds of British subjects, a large proportion of them ex-Servicemen, were suddenly arrested and thrown into prison under Regulation 18B.

For some days the entire press had been conducting a whirlwind campaign, in rising crescendo, against a supposed fifth column in this country, which was declared to be waiting to assist the Germans when they landed.

How untrue this campaign was, is proved by the fact that our most competent Intelligence Service never produced the flimsiest evidence of any such conspiracy, nor evidence of any plan or order relating to it, nor the complicity in such an undertaking of any single man arrested.[14]

---

[14] As you read this, consider the lies about alleged weapons of mass destruction stockpiled by Saddam Hussein, to justify the massacre in Iraq. There were none or they would have been used, yes? And remember G.W. Bush's comment early on, when he was declaring "war on terror": "If you aren't for us, you are against us". So those against the never-ending war are suspected and accused of being terrorists. The more things change, the more they stay the same.

Had such evidence been forthcoming, those implicated would undoubtedly have been charged and tried, and very properly so. But there was not one case of a man arrested under 18B being a British subject, who was so charged.

Four charges were actually framed against one lady, the wife of a distinguished Admiral, Mrs Nicholson. She was tried by a Judge and jury, and acquitted on all counts. This however, did not prevent her being arrested as she left the Law Courts, acquitted, and being thrown into Holloway Prison under Regulation 18B, where she remained for years.

Regulation 18B was originally introduced to deal with certain members of the I.R.A., who were committing a number of senseless minor outrages in London. Without this Regulation, no liege of His Majesty in the United Kingdom could be arrested and held in prison on suspicion.

This practice had long been abandoned in this country, except in short periods of grave proven conspiracy, and on those occasions Habeas Corpus was always suspended.

18B enabled the medieval process of arrest and imprisonment on suspicion to be revived without the suspension of Habeas Corpus. It was, in fact, a return to the system of Lettres de Cachet, by which persons in pre-Revolutionary France were consigned to the Bastille.

Here, it should be remembered, that those persons enjoyed full social intercourse with their families, and were allowed their own servants, plate, linen, food and drink whilst in prison; a very different treatment to that meted out to persons held under 18B, whose treatment for some time was little different from ordinary criminals, and, in fact, worse than any remand prisoner.

These I.R.A. outrages were so fatuous in themselves and so apparently meaningless, at a time when there were no sharp differences between this country and the Irish Free State, that I commenced making a number of inquiries.

I was not surprised to discover at length, that special members of the I.R.A. had been enrolled for the committing of these outrages; and that they were practically all Communists.

I had it on excellent authority that the Left Book Club of Dublin had been actively concerned in the matter; and finally the names of 22 of these men were put into my hands; and again I was informed on excellent authority that they were **all Communists**.

Immediately on receipt of this information I put down a question to the Home Secretary, and offered to supply the necessary information if the matter were taken up. Nothing came of my representations. **From these Communist-inspired outrages, however, there resulted Regulation 18B.**[15]

Though the I.R.A. were pleaded as an excuse to the House for a Regulation, hardly any of their members were ever arrested under it; but in due course it was

---

[15] And today, we get the U.S.A. Patriot Act, by the same methods, and for the same reason. To squelch truth and the truth-sayers.

employed to arrest and hold for 4 or 5 years, uncharged, very many hundreds of British subjects, whose one common denominator was that they opposed the Jewish power over this country in general; and its exertion to thrust her into a war in purely Jewish interests in particular.

Now Communism is Jewish-controlled.

If Marxist Jewry needed a device for securing the assent of parliament to a regulation like 18B, what simpler method could there be to achieve this object, without arousing suspicion as to the real **ulterior motive**, than arranging for a few communist members of the I.R.A. to plant bombs in the cloakrooms of London stations?

Everyone is supposed to be entitled to their opinion in this country; and, furthermore, where we cannot supply absolute proof, we can say with the Home Secretary, as I do here, that I have "reasonable cause to believe" that this is the real story behind Regulation 18B's enactment.

When the Clause was first introduced into the House, the original wording laid it down quite clearly that the Home Secretary should have the power to detain persons of British birth and origin "If he was satisfied that" such detention was necessary. This terminology was, at least, crystal clear.

No other opinion or check upon the Home Secretary's personal and absolute discretion was envisaged: a return, in fact and in very essence, to the Lettres de Cachet and the Star Chamber. The House of Commons refused absolutely to accept such a clause, or hand away its powers of supervision, and its responsibilities as the guardian of the rights and liberties of the citizen to any individual, be the Cabinet Minister or not.

The Government accordingly had to withdraw the offending sentence; and brought forward a second draft for approval some days later. In this new draft, drawn up, as Government spokesmen laboured to explain, in accordance with the express wishes of the House, the necessary safeguard from arbitrary executive tyranny had been introduced.

For the words "Home Secretary is satisfied that," had been substituted, "Has reasonable cause to believe that."

The Government spokesmen explained at length on this occasion that this wording gave the required safeguard. Members of Parliament were led to believe that their wishes had prevailed, and that they were to be the judges of what would or would not be "Reasonable Cause" for continued detention (as was proved in subsequent debates), and a rather uneasy House passed the Clause in this form, and on that understanding.

Two years later, when the Counsel of an 18B prisoner argued in Court along these lines, and demanded some sort of ventilation of his client's case before Members of Parliament or a Court, no less a person than the Attorney-General himself pleaded on the Government's behalf, that the words "Has reasonable cause to believe that," meant precisely the same as "Is satisfied that."

There the matter had to rest as far as the Law Courts were concerned, though it was the subject of the most scathing comment of a most eminent Law Lord.

I myself was arrested under this Regulation on 23rd May, 1940, and thrown into Brixton Prison, where I remained in a cell until 26th September, 1944, without any charge being preferred against me, receiving merely a curt notification from the Home Office on the latter date that the order for my detention had been "revoked."

A paper of "Particulars" alleged as the reasons for my detention was supplied to me soon after my arrest. I replied to them during a day's interrogation by the so-called Advisory Committee, before which body I could call no witnesses, did not know who were my accusers, or the accusations they had made, and was not allowed the assistance of a lawyer.

These particulars, together with my detailed reply to each, were set out in part II of a Statement I supplied later to the Speaker and Members of the House of Commons; and will be found in the Appendix of this book. They were based upon the untrue assertion that my anti-Communist attitude was bogus, and a cloak for disloyal activities.

How untrue this slander was can be easily proved from my previous ten years' record of unceasing attacks on Communism, both by questions and speeches in the House of Commons and outside.

WHO DARES?

On the morning following my release from Brixton Prison, I proceeded to the House of Commons at my usual hour of 10.15 a.m.; an action which appeared to cause no little surprise. It was not long before Jews and their friends were on my trail, and that of the Right Club.

A string of provocative questions soon appeared on the Order Paper; but, like Gallio who, when the Jews took Sosthenes, and beat him before the Judgment seat, "cared for none of these things," I gave no sign of interest. The reporters in the Press Galleries were then turned on, to endeavour to extract from me some, at least, of the names in 'the Red Book' of the Right Club membership.

Now the names in the Red Book of members of the Right Club were, as the newspapers have shrieked aloud, kept strictly private, with the sole object of preventing the names becoming known to the Jews. The sole reason for this privacy was the expressed wish of the members themselves.

To me, personally, the keeping of the names secret was only a disadvantage. It facilitated misrepresentation of every kind by my enemies; the publication of the names would have been of great assistance to me in every way.

The sole reason for this stipulation on joining by so many members was the well-grounded fear of Jewish retaliation of a serious nature.

I remember in particular the conversation on this subject with one of these reporters from the Press Gallery of the House of Commons. He was an engaging young man, and particularly importunate. Would I not let him have just a few of the names? I said to him:

> "Supposing your name had been amongst those in the Red Book; and supposing that in disregard of my promise to you not to reveal it, I proceeded to communicate it to the press; and supply that definite evidence that you were a member of a society to fight against Jewish domination over Britain: you would not keep your job with your paper for six months."

"I shouldn't keep it for six minutes," was the prompt reply.

"Exactly," I answered. "Now you can see why I can't give you the name of even one member of the Right Club from the Red Book. You yourself confirm their worst fears."

Many hundreds of poor fellows find themselves in such a position today; indeed, hundreds is merely a matter of expression. The real number must be prodigious. How many, one might ask, can afford to run the risk to their livelihood, which is involved in letting it be known that they are aware of the Jewish grip and prepared to oppose it.

Even the wealthiest and most influential magnates of the

land dare not brave the wrath of organised Jewry as the story regarding the *Daily Mail* controlling shares on pp. 6 and 7 of my statement to the Speaker shows.

Not only in Britain has this been the case, but perhaps even more noticeably in the U.S.A., as the diaries of the late Mr James Forrestal prove.

The Forrestal Diaries published by the Viking Press, New York, 1951, only reach me as this book goes to press. Coming from a man of high integrity, who was U.S. Navy Under Secretary from 1940, and Secretary for Defence from 1947 until his resignation and suspicious death a few days later in March 1949, they are of the utmost significance. The most important revelation therein is dated the 27th December, 1945 (pages 121 and 122):

> "Played golf today with Joe Kennedy (Joseph P. Kennedy, who was Roosevelt's Ambassador to Great Britain in the years immediately before the war). I asked him about his conversations with Roosevelt and Neville Chamberlain from 1938 on. He said Chamberlain's position in 1938 was that England had nothing with which to fight and that she could not risk going to war with Hitler.
>
> Kennedy's view: That Hitler would have fought Russia without any later conflict with England if it had not been for Bullitt's (William C. Bullitt - a half-Jew - then Ambassador to France) urging on Roosevelt in the summer of 1939 that the Germans must be faced down about Poland; neither the French nor the British would have made Poland a cause of war if it had not been for the constant needling from Washington.

> Bullitt, he said, kept telling Roosevelt that the Germans wouldn't fight, Kennedy that they would, and that they would overrun Europe. Chamberlain, he said, stated that America and the world Jews had forced England into the war."

If Mr Forrestal's information regarding the impulses behind the recent war needed any confirmation, they have already had it from the outspoken statements of Mr. Oswald Pirow, former South African Defence Minister, who told the Associated Press on the 14th January, 1952, in Johannesburg that:

> "Chamberlain had told him that he was under great pressure from World Jewry not to accommodate Hitler."

A second most important revelation in the Forrestal Diaries concerns Zionism. It is clear from the entries, that by December, 1947, Mr. Forrestal was becoming greatly concerned by the intervention of the Zionists into American politics. He records conversations with Mr. Byrnes and Senator Vandenberg, Governor Dewey and others, in attempts to lift the Palestine question out of party politics. From this time on he would seem to have made continuous efforts with that end in view.

The Diary records on the 3rd Feb., 1948 (pages 362 and 363):

> "Visit today from Franklin D. Roosevelt Jr., who came in with strong advocacy of a Jewish State in Palestine, that we should support the United Nations 'decision', I pointed out that the United Nations had as yet taken no 'decision', that it was only a recommendation of the General Assembly and that I thought the methods that

> had been used by people outside of the Executive branch of the Government to bring coercion and duress on other nations in the General Assembly bordered closely onto scandal...
>
> I said I was merely directing my efforts to lifting the question out of politics, that is, to have the two parties agree that they would not compete for votes on this issue.
>
> He said this was impossible, that the nation was too far committed and that, furthermore, the Democratic Party would be bound to lose and the Republicans gain by such an agreement.
>
> I said I was forced to repeat to him what I had said to Senator McGrath in response to the latter's observation that our failure to go along with the Zionists might lose the states of New York, Pennsylvania and California - that I thought it was about time that somebody should pay some consideration to whether we might not lose the United States."

After a short note by the Editor of the Diaries the entry for the 3rd Feb., 1948, continues (page 364):

> "Had lunch with Mr. B. M. Baruch. After lunch raised the same question with him. He took the line of advising me not to be active in this particular matter, and that I was already identified, to a degree that was not in my own interest, with opposition to the United Nations policy on Palestine."

It was about this time that a campaign of unparalleled slander and calumny was launched in the United States press and periodicals against Mr. Forrestal. So greatly did this appear to have affected him that in March 1949, he resigned from the U.S. Defence Secretaryship; and on the 22nd of that month was found dead as a result of a fall from a very high window.

EPILOGUE

I shall always be grateful to the many Members who made my return to the House very much easier than it might have been, by their immediate greetings and friendly attitude.

Many, I fear, whose actions in the Chamber itself and outside were detected or reported to the press representatives, found themselves the victims of a vendetta inside their constituencies and in the Press on that specific account.

When we reflect upon these bloody happenings from the time of King Charles I to our own day, we can at long last find only one cause for satisfaction, if such a word can be in any way appropriate. It is that for the first time we can now trace the underlying influences, which explain these hideous disfigurations in European history.

In the light of present-day knowledge, we can now recognise and understand the true significance of these terrible happenings. Instead of mere disconnected occurrences, we can now discern the merciless working of a satanic plan; and seeing and understanding, we are in a position to take steps in the future to safeguard all those values, which we love and stand for; and which that plan clearly seeks to destroy.

We can at last begin to oppose the planners and operators of that plan, knowing about it and their technique, which till now have been known to them alone. In other words, being fore-warned, it is our fault if we are not fore-armed.

Let us not forget such words as those of the Jew Marcus Eli Ravage, who wrote in the *Century Magazine* U.S.A. in January 1928:

> "We have stood back of, not only the last war, but all your wars; and not only the Russian, but all of your revolutions worthy of mention in your history."

Nor should we forget those of Professor Harold Laski, writing in the *New Statesman and Nation* on 11th January, 1942:

> "For this war is in its essence merely an immense revolution in which the war of 1914, the Russian Revolution, and the counter revolutions on the Continent are earlier phases."

Nor the warning from that eminent Jewish American Attorney, publisher and reporter, Henry Klein, issued only last year:

> "The Protocols is the plan by which a handful of Jews, who compose the Sanhedrin, aim to rule the world by first destroying Christian civilisation."

> "Not only are the Protocols genuine, in my opinion, but they have been almost entirely fulfilled."

They have indeed been largely fulfilled; no small measure of Jewish thanks being due to Mr. Roosevelt and his "ardent lieutenant," the self-styled "architect of the Jewish future."

In the process, however, Britain and her Empire and, worse still, her good name and honour have been brought down to the dust. As Professor Beard wrote:

> "The noble principles of the Four Freedoms and the Atlantic Charter were for practical purposes discarded in the settlements which accompanied the progress and followed the conclusion of the war. In the validity of this statement the treatment of the people of Esthonia, Lithuania, Poland, Roumania, Yugoslavia, China, Indo-China, Indonesia, Italy, Germany and other places of the earth bear witness."

There appeared recently in the press the cry of Mrs. Chiang Kai Shek calling Britain a "moral weakling" (in reference to China). She is reported as saying:

> "Britain has bartered the soul of a nation for a few pieces of silver... One day these pieces of silver will bear interest in British blood, toil, sweat and tears on the battleground of freedom."

It might be General Sikorski himself speaking, might it not? In the same paper I saw that Mr. Jackson Martindell, president of the American Institute of Management, has declared that,

> "an Englishman's word is no longer his bond."

How often have I heard this from Arab sources since 1939? Mr. Martindell continued,

> "I hate to say this, but Britain is becoming poor morally

as well as economically."

From Poland to Palestine and to China these words are re-echoed, and be it said, reiterated by the Jew-wise section of this country for many years.

The reason is not far to seek. No man can serve two masters, more especially when the principles and interests of these two masters are as widely divergent as are those of Britain and her Empire, and Jewry and their Empire, the U.S.S.R.

Ever since the fall of Mr. Chamberlain's Government, the interests of the Jewish Empire have been advanced as prodigiously as those of Britain and her Empire have been eclipsed.

Stranger than all this - should any dare to state the truth in plain terms-the only response is an accusation of anti-Semitism. As Mr. Douglas Reed has clearly shown, the term "anti-Semitism" is meaningless rubbish - and as he suggests it might as well be called "anti-Semolina."

The Arabs are Semites, and no so-called "anti-Semite" is anti-Arab. It is not even correct to say that he is anti-Jew. On the contrary, he knows better than the uninformed that a fair proportion of Jews are not engaged in this conspiracy.

The only correct term for the miscalled "anti-Semitic" is "Jew-wise". It is indeed the only fair and honest term.

The phrase "anti-Semite" is merely a propaganda word used to stampede the unthinking public into dismissing the whole subject from their minds without examination:

so long as that is tolerated these evils will not only continue, but grow worse.

The "Jew-wise" know that we have in Britain a Jewish "Imperium in Imperio," which, in spite of all protestations and camouflage, is Jewish first and foremost, and in complete unison with the remainder of World Jewry. If any doubt this they need only read *Unity in Dispersion*, issued in 1948 by the World Jewish Congress, which proclaims Jewry to be one nation.

Not all Jews here wish to be railroaded into this narrow social tyranny; but unless this country affords them some way of escape they dare not take the risks - very grave risks - of defying it: and so they perforce co-operate to some degree.

Even worse, certain Gentiles with no good excuse support this united force, which is in turn used to influence or control our political parties, home and foreign policies, press and public life.

This unholy united front must be exposed and frustrated. One step towards this objective would seem to be firstly an enactment to prevent Gentile Esaus from lending their hands for the carrying out of orders uttered by the voice of Jewish Jacobs.

Another: the detachment from the Jewish United Front of Jews, who do not wish to subscribe to the dictates of the World Jewish Congress. First and foremost however is the need to inform people of good will as to the truth of this matter, particularly in regard to the real anatomy, aims, and methods of the Marxist enemy.

It is to that end, that I humbly offer the contents of this book to all, who are determined to fight Communism.

STATEMENT

STATEMENT BY CAPT. RAMSAY FROM BRIXTON PRISON TO THE SPEAKER AND MEMBERS OF PARLIAMENT CONCERNING HIS DETENTION UNDER PARAGRAPH 18B OF THE DEFENCE REGULATIONS.

All the particulars alleged as grounds for my detention are based on charges that my attitude and activities in opposition to Communism, Bolshevism, and the policy of organised Jewry were not genuine, but merely a camouflage for anti-British designs.

In the following memorandum, which could be greatly expanded, I have given a minimum of facts, which prove that not only was my attitude genuine, open, and unvarying during the whole of my time in the House of Commons, but that in the course of my researches I had accumulated numerous and conclusive facts compelling such an attitude, and leading logically to the formation of the Right Club, an essentially patriotic organisation.

During the whole of my time as M.P. (since 1931) I have kept up an open and unremitting attack on Bolshevism and its allies. Indeed, I had already started this opposition long before I became an M.P.

The following survey will show this; and also the eventual formation of the Right Club as the logical outcome of my work.

This work falls into three phases.

During the first, dating from soon after the Russian Revolution till about 1935, I supposed the powers behind Bolshevism to be Russian: In the second (1935-38) I appreciated that they were International: By the third phase, I realised them to be Jewish.

PHASE I

It was always a mystery to me in Phase I why Russians spent so much time and money on revolutionary activities in Britain.

My first active step was to speak in the election made famous by the publication in the *Daily Mail* of the letter written by Zinoviev alias Apfelbaum, calling for revolution in Britain. (I spoke against Bolshevism, and in the Northwich division.)

On being elected in 1931, I joined the Russian Trade Committee, which kept a watch on their activities here. I also joined the Council of the Christian Protest Movement, founded to protest against the outrages on priests, nuns, and the Christian churches committed by the Bolsheviks. Hansard will show that I asked many questions during this period, attacking their activities in this country.

PHASE II

In Phase II, I recognised the forces behind Bolshevism not to be Russian, but international.

I tried to picture the composition of that mysterious body, the Comintern, over whom, according to the replies to my Parliamentary questions, the Soviet Government could exercise no control.

In the latter end of this phase I had made sufficient progress with this mental picture of the Comintern, that I made it the subject of a number of addresses, which I gave to Rotary Clubs and other societies in London, Edinburgh, and elsewhere, entitling them frequently, "Red Wings Over Europe."

This second phase lasted well into the Spanish Civil War. Recognising almost at once the guilt of the Comintern in the whole affair, down to the International Brigade, I attacked them continuously by a stream of questions in the House.

The attitude of the entire British national Press at first amazed, and subsequently helped to enlighten me, as to the real powers behind World Revolution. **The press presented General Franco's enemies as liberal and Protestant reformers, instead of the anti-God international revolutionaries they were.**

Officials of the Russian Cheka were actually in charge of the prisons on the Red side. McGovern established all the main facts in his pamphlet, *Red Terror in Spain*.

I organised parades of sandwich-men at this time to expose the Bolshevik guilt in Spain, assisted a paper called *The Free Press*, and did what propaganda I could. Some eighty or ninety M.P.s subscribed at one time or another to these efforts.

In September 1937 I accepted the Chairmanship of the United Christian Front Committee, on behalf of Sir Henry Lunn.

Thereafter many thousands of letters were sent out over my signature to leading people in the Kingdom, appraising them of the true facts of the war in Spain, and urging Christians of all communities to join in combating the Godless Red Terror, that threatened Spain then, and thereafter all Europe, Britain included.

A number of patriotic societies now began to co-operate regularly with me in this work against Bolshevism, including the National Citizens' Union, the British Empire League, the Liberty Restoration League, and the Economic League. We took to meeting regularly in a Committee Room of the House of Commons.

In May 1936, when I set out to oppose the entry into this country of agents of the Comintern for attending the so-called Godless Congress, we were joined by the British Bible Union, the Order of the Child, and the British Israel World Federation.

From information given me by these societies, I realized that the previous Godless Congress, held at Prague, had brought under unified control all the National Free-Thinker societies, who were now under the authority of the Militant Godless of Russia, and were therefore a subtle and potent weapon for Bolshevik propaganda.

At our meetings to co-ordinate opposition, we all agreed that while it was perhaps the right of British men and women to hold a Congress on any subject, this liberty should not be construed into licence for international revolutionaries to develop their plans for the destruction of the religious, social and public life of our country.

On the 28th June, therefore, I introduced a Bill entitled the ALIENS' RESTRICTION (BLASPHEMY) BILL, to prevent aliens from attending this Congress, or making it the occasion for the distribution of their blasphemous literature.

The Bill received a first reading by 165 votes to 134. In the No Lobby were Messrs. Rothschild, G.R. Strauss, T. Levy, A.M. Lyons, Sir F. Harris, D.N. Pritt, W. Gallacher, Dr. Haden Guest and Dr. Summerskill.

In the **autumn of 1938** I was made acquainted with the fact that the power behind World Revolution was not just a vague body of internationalists, but organized World Jewry.

The first document so convincing me was actually a British Government White Paper, of whose existence I had not been previously aware. This quoted verbatim an extract from a report received by Mr. Balfour on September 19th, 1918, from Mr. Oudendyke, the Netherlands Minister in Petrograd, who was at that time in charge of British interests there, as follows:

> "The danger is now so great, that I feel it my duty to call the attention of the British Government and all other Governments to the fact that if an end is not put to Bolshevism at once the civilization of the whole world will be threatened. This is not an exaggeration, but a matter of fact...
>
> I consider that the immediate suppression of

> Bolshevism is the greatest issue before the world, not even excluding the war which is still raging, and unless as above stated Bolshevism is nipped in the bud immediately it is bound to spread over Europe and the whole world in one form or another, as it is organized and worked by Jews, who have no nationality and whose one object it is to destroy for their own ends the existing order of things. The only manner in which this danger can be averted would be collective action on the part of all the Powers."

Almost as remarkable as the above quotation was the fact brought to my notice simultaneously, namely, that this White Paper had been immediately withdrawn, and replaced by an abridged edition, from which these vital passages had been eliminated. I was shown the two White papers-the original and the abridged issue, side by side.

The second document which came to my notice at this time was the booklet entitled, *The Rulers of Russia*, written by Dr. Dennis Fahey, C.S.S.P., and bearing the imprimatur of the Archbishop of Dublin, dated the 26th March, 1938. In the opening sentence of this pamphlet Dr Fahey writes:

> "In this pamphlet I present to my readers a number of serious documents which go to show that the real forces behind Bolshevism are Jewish forces; and that Bolshevism is really an instrument in the hands of the Jews for the establishment of their future Messianic kingdom."

Dr. Fahey then adduces an interesting volume of evidence. On page 1 he gives also the following passage by Mr. Hilaire Belloc, taken from the latter's Weekly, dated 4th February, 1937:

> "As for anyone who does not know that the present revolutionary Bolshevist movement in Russia is Jewish, I can only say that he must be a man who is taken in by the suppression of our deplorable Press."

Other authorities quoted in the pamphlet include Dr. Homer, D. Sc., Count Leon de Poncins in his *Contre-Revolution*, and evidence given on 12th February, 1919, before a Committee of the United States Senate by the Rev. George A. Simons, Superintendent of the Methodist Episcopal Church in Petrograd from 1907 to October 6th 1918.

The Rev. Mr. Simons stated on this occasion with regard to the Bolshevik Government in Petrograd:

> "In December 1918... under the Presidency of a man known as Apfelbaum (Zinoviev)... out of 388 members, only 16 happened to be real Russians, and all the rest (with the exception of one man, who is a Negro from North America) were Jews... and 265 of these Jews belonging to this Northern Commune Government that is sitting in the old Smolny Institute come from the Lower East Side of New York -- 265 of them."

On page 8 Dr Fahey quotes figures showing that in the year 1936:

> "The Central Committee of the Communist Party in Moscow, the very centre of International Communism, consisted of 59 members, of whom 56 were Jews, and the other three were married to Jewesses..."

"Stalin, present ruler of Russia, is not a Jew, but he took

as his second wife the twenty-one year old sister of the Jew L.M. Kaganovitch, his right-hand man, who has been spoken of as his probable or possible successor. Stalin's every movement is made under Jewish eyes."

In addition to these documents there now reached me a quantity of evidence concerning Jewish activities in Great Britain in the shape of subversive organizations of every description, anti-religious, anti-moral, revolutionary, and those working to establish the Jewish system of financial and industrial monopoly.

Thus I became finally convinced of the fact that the Russian and Spanish revolutions, and the subversive societies in Britain, were part and parcel of the one and the same Plan, secretly operated and controlled by World Jewry, exactly on the lines laid down in the *Protocols of the Elders of Zion*, filed in the British Museum in 1906 (which had been reproduced soon after the last war by *The Morning Post*, and from which this newspaper never recovered).

These Protocols are no forgery, and I and others could supply evidence to that effect that would convince any impartial Tribunal.

At the next meeting of the patriotic and Christian societies, I felt in duty bound to broach the Jewish question; and realized, very soon, that there had come a parting of the ways. With very few exceptions our co-operation ceased.

I realized that if anything was to be done, some special group would have to be formed which, while retaining the essential characteristics of the former one, would take up the task of opposing and exposing the Jewish menace. It was then that the idea of the Right Club originated, though the actual formation did not actually come about till some months later, in May 1939.

From the autumn of 1938 onwards, I spent many hours a week talking to back- benchers and members of the Government alike on these subjects.

The very magnitude of the issues involved put many off. One particular rejoinder typifies in my recollection this sort of attitude:

> "Well, that is all very disturbing, awful, in fact: but what is one to do about it? I shall go off now and try and forget all about it as soon as possible."

About the **end of 1938**, news was brought to me that the control shares of the *Daily Mail* were for sale.

Knowing that a severe advertisement boycott had been put in operation against the paper following upon its having printed two or three articles giving what in Internationalist eyes had been a pro-Franco view of the Spanish War (in reality, the truth), the news was no great surprise to me.

Could I find a buyer? I decided to approach a certain very wealthy and patriotic peer, the head of a great business. A mutual friend arranged an interview.

On introduction I gave a survey of the activities and power of Organized Jewry in general, and of their secret publicity control in Britain in particular, as I saw it. When I ended after some 70 minutes, general concurrence in my views was expressed.

Thereupon the mutual friend and I tried to persuade our hearer to buy the said shares and "tear the gag off the conspiracy of silence." He replied:

> "I daren't. They would bring me to a crust of bread. If it was only myself, I wouldn't mind; I'd fight them. But many of my shares are held by the widow and the orphan, and for their sakes I must refuse."

On our expressing astonishment that Jewry could inflict such crushing retaliation on a man of his financial strength and industrial power, and so conspicuous a national figure, he gave us details of just such retaliation directed against him by Organized Jewry some years previously.

He had refused to comply with some demands they had made of him affecting his works. After a final warning, which he ignored, a world boycott had been started against him, which had become effective in 24 hours, wherever he had agents or offices. Fires and strikes also mysteriously occurred. The resulting losses had finally compelled him to give in.

Within 24 hours the boycott was lifted all over the world.

The consistent misreporting of important features in the Spanish Civil War had deeply impressed many M.P.s They felt that a bias so extreme, so universal, and so consistent, always against Franco, indicated the existence of some deliberate plan, and though unwilling to agree my thesis, that the Jews were operating this control by various means, and that the whole affair was part of their World Plan, nevertheless many felt that something was very wrong somewhere.

In the course of these conversations I obtained the support of Members of all parties to the Bill I was preparing in this connection.

On **December 13th, 1938**, I introduced the Bill entitled COMPANIES ACT AMENDMENT BILL, which made it compulsory for shares in Newspapers and News Agencies to be held in the actual names of the holders, instead of the names of nominees as is done now in the majority of cases.

The Bill received a First Reading by 151 votes to 104. In the Aye Lobby were Members of all parties, including 13 Right Hon. Gentlemen 98 of these Socialists).

In the No Lobby were Messrs. Rothschild, Schuster, Shinwell, Cazalet, Gallacher, Sir A. Sinclair, Gluckstein, and Mr. Samuel Storey opposed, also blocked the Bill; and seemed suitable for that role.

I now took the decision to proceed at once with the formation of a group similar in character to the group of representatives of Christian and patriotic societies, which I had worked with up to the emergence of the Jewish problem; but this time a group which would place opposition to that menace in the forefront of its activities.

Mr. Cross was the Secretary, and the late duke of Wellington, President of the Liberty Restoration League, was the Chairman at most of the few meetings we held. The first object of the Right Club was to enlighten the Tory Party and clear it from any Jewish control.

Organized Jewry was now clearly out for World War. The failure of their International Brigade in Spain, and the growing exposure of themselves, and the consequent risk of total collapse of their plan rendered immediate war from their point of view imperative.

In **July 1939** I had an interview with the Prime Minister. I dealt with the Russian Revolution, and the part Jewry had played in it; and with the Spanish Revolution, prepared and carried out on similar lines by much the same people; with the subversive societies in Britain, and the Press and news control existing in this country.

I finally drew the Prime Minister's attention to the underground work that was going on with the object of overthrowing his peace policy and himself, and precipitating the war.

Mr Chamberlain considered that charges of so grave and far-reaching a character would require very substantial documentary proof. I decided to collect documentary proof which would make it possible for action to be taken.

The outbreak of war enabled the Jews to give their activities the cloak of patriotism. Their press power enabled them to portray those opposing their designs and exposing them as pro-Nazi, and disloyal to Britain.

The difficulty I was faced with was that while I was in duty bound to warn the country against the consequences of a policy influenced by Organized Jewry and opposed to British interests, I, at the same time, did not want to create difficulties for Mr Chamberlain.

It was decided therefore, that the Right Club should close down for the duration. The spirit of the Club naturally led the younger members to join the Services, wherein they have served with distinction on most fronts. It was in keeping with the same spirit that others not so engaged, should continue to fight the internal enemy, no less formidable than the Axis Powers and in a way more dangerous, owing to his secret methods and the fact that he can work from within as well as from without.

To this end, therefore, I and others in an individual capacity disseminated on occasion some leaflets of mine called Do You Know? and Have You Noticed?; my verses beginning "Land of dope and Jewry", and some anti-Jewish stickers. This was with the idea of educating the public sufficiently to maintain the atmosphere in which the "phoney" war, as it was called, might be converted into an honourable negotiated peace.

It was certainly not defeatist, as Jewish propaganda tried to make out. It was not we of the Right Club who were holding back from the fighting Services in this war, any more than in that last; quite the contrary.

I was determined to make further efforts to convince Mr. Chamberlain, and even perhaps the 1922 Committee, of the truth of my case, and thus avert total war, and commenced reinforcing the documentary evidence already in my possession.

By **January 1940**, I had details of nearly thirty subversive societies working on various revolutionary and corrosive lines, and had completed a very large chart, showing the principal members of each. Six names stood out clearly, as a sort of interlocking directorate. They were Prof. H. Laski, Mr. Israel Moses Sieff, Prof. Herman Levy, Mr. Victor Gollancz, Mr. D.N. Pritt, M.P., and Mr. G.R. Strauss, M.P.

In February 1940, on my arrival in London, I was handed the literature of a new group, who were advocating FEDERAL UNION. The list of supporters' names was startling. It might have been copied from the chart I had just completed. There could be no mistake as to the source of this scheme. Later, when this group became active, I put down the following questions:

Captain Ramsay asked the Prime Minister whether he could assure the House that the creation of a Federal Union of the European States is not one of the war aims of H.M.'s Government.

Mr. Butler (on May 9th) gave a non-committal reply. To this I asked the following supplementary:

Captain Ramsey: Is my right Hon. Friend aware that this plan, if adopted, will arouse hostility against us in almost the whole of Europe, who look upon it as the setting up of a Judeo-Masonic super-State?[16]

Mr. Butler: I would rather leave my Hon. Friend's interpretation of this plan to him.

A virulent Press campaign was now in full swing to

---

[16] *The Protocols of the Elders of Zion* make it clear that World Jewry and Orient Masonry will set up just such a regime after the Gentile States have been reduced by War and Revolutions to hewers of wood and drawers of water.

suppress "Anti-Semitic" views and activities by declaring that "Anti-Semitism" was pro-Nazi. Fearing less the Home Secretary might be inclined into this direction, which was a false direction, I asked him on May 9th, 1940:

Captain Ramsay: Whether he will give an assurance that care will be taken, both in the administration of the present regulations, and in framing revised ones, that a distinction is made between anti-Semitism and pro-Nazism?

Sir J. Anderson: I hope that any restrictive measures applied to organized propaganda may in practice be confined to such propaganda as is calculated to impede the war effort; and from that point of view I cannot recognize as relevant the distinction which My. Hon. and Gallant Friend seeks to draw.

Captain Ramsay: while think my Right Hon. Friend for his reply, in view of the fact that he seems somewhat confused on this point, will he assure the House that he refuses to be stampeded into identifying the two things by a ramp in our Jew-ridden press?

Sir J. Anderson: There is no question of my being stampeded into anything.

It was in the last weeks of Mr. Chamberlain's Premiership that I was enabled to look through some of the U.S. Embassy papers at Mr. Kent's flat. This then was the position, and these were the considerations which led me to inspect them.

1. Together with many members of both Houses of

Parliament, I was fully aware that among the agencies here and abroad, which had been actively engaged in promoting bad feeling between Great Britain and Germany, Organized Jewry, for obvious reasons, had played a leading part.

2. I knew the U.S.A. to be the headquarters of Jewry, and therefore the real, though not apparent, centre of their activity.

3. I was aware that Federal Union was the complement in international affairs of the scheme of Political and Economic Planning (P.E.P.). The Chairman of P.E.P. is Mr. Israel Moses Sieff, who is also Vice-Chairman of the Zionist Federation and Grand Commander of the Order of Maccabeans) designed to bring about Bolshevism by stealth in the sphere of industry and commerce, and that it must be regarded as the Super-State, which is one of the principal objectives of International Jewry.

4. I recognized that plans for establishing Marxist Socialism under Jewish control in this country were far advanced. As to their intentions, there could be no doubt.

5. I knew that the technique of International Jewry is always to plan the overthrow at critical junctures of any national leader who seriously opposes some essential part of their designs, as for instance Mr. Chamberlain had done by adhering to his policy of pacification, and that in this case Mr. Chamberlain's fall would precipitate total war. I remembered that Mr. Lloyd George had said in the House of Commons, that if we were let in for a war over Poland without the help of Russia, we should be walking into a trap. We walked into that trap.

Further information as to its origin, design, and

ultimate objective, would have strengthened Mr. Chamberlain's hand, and would have enabled him to take the appropriate counter-measures. As a Member of Parliament, still loyal to Mr. Chamberlain, I considered it my duty to investigate.

About the 9th or 10th of May I went to Scotland for a fortnight's rest, having seen only a part of the documents, and intending to resume my investigations on my return. Before I could conclude them, however, Mr. Chamberlain had fallen from office, and I was arrested a few days later on the steps of my house, when I returned to London on the 23rd May, 1940.

I am appending the Particulars, alleged as Reasons for my detention, and my comments thereon.

Brixton Prison, August 23rd, 1943

(Signed) ARCHIBALD RAMSAY.

PARTICULARS ALLEGED AS REASONS FOR MY DETENTION

There follows here a copy of the Particulars, which were alleged to be reasonable grounds for my detention for the last three years.

It will be seen that the whole basis of every one of them is, that my opposition to Communism, Bolshevism and World Jewry was but a sham; a disloyal ruse, in fact, adopted to mask anti-British activities in relation to the war.

Anyone conversant with doings in the House of Commons will be more or less familiar with the anti-Bolshevik activities that I have kept up openly and consistently all through my time in the House since 1931; and which activities became anti-Jewish in 1938, when I realized that Bolshevism was Jewish and an integral part of their World Plan.

The framer of these Particulars brushes aside the whole of that eight years' record, and proceeds to fabricate and reiterate some new and disloyal purpose, for which slanders he offers no shred of substantiation.

Home Office Advisory Committee
(Defence Regulation 18B) London, W.1.
Telephone: Regent 4784 Ref.:... R4...
24th June, 1940

REASONS FOR ORDER MADE UNDER DEFENCE REGULATION 18B IN THE CASE OF CAPTAIN ARCHIBALD MAULE RAMSAY, M.P.

The Order under Defence Regulation 18B was made against Captain Archibald Maule Ramsay, M.P. Because the Secretary of State had reasonable cause to believe that the said Captain Archibald Maule RAMSAY, M.P. had been recently concerned in acts prejudicial to the public safety or the defence of the Realm, or in the preparation or instigation of such acts, and that by reason thereof it was necessary to exercise control over him.[17]

PARTICULARS

The said Captain Archibald Maule RAMSAY, M.P.

Particular (i): In or about the month of May 1939,

---

[17] Notice that ONE Person, had "reasonable cause to believe", and under that clause, Captain Ramsay was imprisoned for two and a half years. That exact language is codified in the U.S. Criminal Code today. Who do you suppose is 'writing the proposed laws' for the U.S. Congress to rubber stamp? And, bear in mind that the U.S.A. Patriot Act as well as the 'new' Department of Homeland Security was laying in wait for the WTC genocidal act of September 11th, 2001 (known now as 911) planned by the same creatures, and implemented by - who knows who? Their 'minions' and 'lackeys' and those who are damned to a hell of their own making.

formed an Organisation under the name of the "Right Club", which ostensibly directed its activities against Jews, Freemasons and Communists. This Organisation, in reality, was designed secretly to spread subversive and defeatist views among the civil population of Great Britain, to obstruct the war effort of Great Britain, and thus to endanger public safety and the defence of the Realm.

Reply

The formation of the Right Club, as the attached memorandum shows, was the logical outcome of many years of work against Bolshevism, carried on both inside and outside the House of Commons, and well-known to all my political colleagues since 1931.

The main object of the Right Club was to oppose and expose the activities of Organized Jewry, in the light of the evidence which came into my possession in 1938, some of which is given in the memorandum.

Our first objective was to clear the Conservative Party of Jewish influence, and the character of our membership and meetings were strictly in keeping with this objective. There were no other and secret purposes.

Our hope was to avert war, which we considered to be mainly the work of Jewish intrigue centred in New York. Later, I and many others hoped to turn the "phoney" war into, not total war, but an honourable negotiated peace.

It is difficult to imagine a body of persons less capable of being "subversive" as this Particular suggests, and coupling this charge with the charge of being "defeatist" places this whole Particular in the realm of the ludicrous.

Particular (ii): In furtherance of the real objects of the Organisation, the said RAMSAY allowed the names of the members of the Organisation to be known only to himself, and took great precautions to see that the register of members did not leave his possession or control; and stated that he had taken steps to mislead the Police and the Intelligence Branch of the War Office as to the real activities of the Organisation. These steps were taken to prevent the real purposes of the Organisation being known.

Reply

The real objects of the Right Club being the declared objects, and there being no other objects whatever, the latter part of this Particular is pure fabrication.

There was only one respect in which our aims differed from the Police and M.I., namely, the Jewish question.

Neither Police nor M.I. recognised the Jewish menace. Neither had any machinery for dealing with it, or for withholding information from Jewish members of their personnel.

If names of members of the Club had been placed at the disposal of either of these departments, they would have been seized upon by the Jewish members therein, and reported on to the very quarters from which many members wished them to be withheld.

Particular (iii): Frequently expressed sympathy with the policy and aims of the German Government; and at times expressed his desire to co-operate with the German government in the conquest and subsequent government of Great Britain.

Reply

The latter half of this Particular is a fabrication so preposterous that I propose to treat it with the contempt it deserves.

Lord Marley embroidered this fiction in the Lords a few days after my arrest, insinuating that I had undertaken to be Gauleiter of Scotland under a German occupation of Great Britain.

My solicitors at once invited him to repeat his remarks outside. Needless to say, he did not do so, for there is not a shred of justification for either this Particular or his slanders.

The term "sympathy with the policy and aims of the German Government" is misleading to the verge of dishonesty. It suggests some general agreement or understanding.

Nothing of the kind existed.

I have never been to Germany, and beyond one formal luncheon at their Embassy knew no Germans. What little I had learned about the Nazi system did not appeal to me.

I have never approved of the idea of movements on distantly similar lines being formed in Britain. On the contrary, I disapproved. My view was that the Unionist Party, once enlightened, was the body best suited to take the needful counter-measures to the Jewish plan, and that to do so successfully it did not even need to go outside the powers latent in our Constitution.

In a general way my views concerning German aspirations coincided exactly with those expressed by Lord Lothian in his speech at Chatham House on 29th June, 1937, when he said:

> "Now if the principle of self-determination were applied on behalf of Germany in the way in which it was applied against her, it would mean the re-entry of Austria into Germany, the union of the Sudeten-Deutch, Danzig and possibly Memel with Germany, and certain adjustments with Poland in Silesia and the Corridor."

The only aspect of the Nazi policy which contacted in any special way with my views was the opposition to the disruptive activities of Organized Jewry. No patriot - British, French, German or of any other nationality - is justified in abandoning the defence of his country to that onslaught, once he has recognized its reality.

To confuse sympathy on this one and loyal point with sympathy with the whole Nazi policy and aims is dishonest; to develop this fallacy into a charge of preferring that system to our own, and being prepared to force that system (of which I disapproved) upon my own country, is the last word in infamy.

Particular (iv): After the formation of the Organisation, made efforts, on behalf of the Organisation, to introduce members of the Organisation into the Foreign Office, the Censorship, the Intelligence Branch of the War Office, and Government departments, in order to further the real objects of the Organisation as set out in (i) hereof.

Reply

Again we have here the fabrication of the wholly unjustifiable charge of a secret and disloyal purpose, already dealt with in Particular (i), and my Memorandum.

In regard to the matter of members of the Right Club and Government offices, I would say this:

The objects of the Club being to spread as rapidly as possible the truth concerning the Jewish danger, time was always a vital factor. From the outset we were in a race with the Jewish propagandists.

To counter them in as many different spheres as possible was obviously the quickest method. Ten members in ten different spheres would spread our information more widely, more quickly than ten members all in the same office or club.

Every political group must follow these lines; this method is the common practice of all political parties.

I never at any time made any effort to get any member a job in any Government Office.

If a member had a choice of two jobs, and didn't mind which he or she took, and asked me about it, I should clearly have replied that as far as the Club was concerned, the sphere in which we had no member to preach the gospel was the one to choose.

For the knowledge to reach such places as the foreign Office, War Office, etc., was obviously to achieve the enlightenment of influential persons most rapidly of all.

Particular (v): After the outbreak of war, associated with and made use of persons known to him to be active in opposition to the interests of Great Britain. Among such persons were one, Anna Wolkoff, and one, Tyler Kent, a Coding Officer employed at the Embassy of the United States of America. With knowledge of the activities in which Wolkoff and Kent were engaged, he continued to associate with them and to make use of their activities on behalf of the "Right Club" and of himself. In particular, with knowledge that Kent had abstracted important documents, the property of the Embassy of the United States of America, he visited Kent's flat at 47, Gloucester Place, where many of the said documents were kept, and inspected them for his own purposes. He further deposited with the said Kent the secret register of the members of the "Right Club", of which Organisation Kent had become an important member, in order to try and keep the nature of the Organisation secret.

Reply

I have never at any time of my life associated with persons whom I have known to be in oppositions to the interests of Britain. On the contrary, my whole record proves that I have devoted more time and trouble than most people to fighting just such persons.

I certainly did not know, and do not now know, that either Mr Kent or Miss Wolkoff were engaged in activities calculated or likely to harm the interests of Britain.

From my own acquaintance with them both, and conversations I have had during that period, I know they both recognized the activities of Organized Jewry to be one of the most evil forces in politics in general, and one of the most dangerous to the interests of Britain in particular.

All their actions will have been directed to countering those Powers and their designs, and most certainly not to anything that might injure the interests of Britain.

As for myself, I should like to add here most emphatically, in view of various mendacious allegations on the subject that have since reached my ears, that I have never, and of course could never contemplate communicating information to enemy quarters.

Having reasonable cause to believe that the Jewish International intrigues to bring about total war radiated from New York, and knowing that activities were being carried on to sabotage Mr Chamberlain's policy of pacification and to bring about his over- throw, it was my obvious duty as a Member of Parliament, and one still loyal to Mr Chamberlain, to make any investigation I could.

I deposited the Red Book of names of the Right Club members at Mr Kent's flat for the period of my absence from London only after I heard of several persons who had had their papers (dealing with the same sort of subjects as mine) ransacked by persons unknown in their absence.

As I have stated already, I had given explicit assurance of privacy to some of the persons whose names were entered therein. Had their names even come into the hands of the British Secret Police, personated as this force is by Jews, their attitude vis-a-vis the Jewish menace would have become known at once in the very quarters from which they made a particular point of their being withheld, namely, Jewish quarters.

Political burglary is no new thing in this country, when one is suspected of possessing information relating to the activities of Organized Jewry.

Lord Craigmyle, when Lord of Appeal, had his whole house ransacked, every drawer broken open and every paper searched without anything being stolen, at a time when it was reasonable to suppose that his papers contained such matter.

The Chief Lieutenant of Police in Edinburgh declared at the time that it was a "political burglary"; the perpetrators were never traced. (See the letter of Lord Craigmyle, dated 6th July, 1920 entitled "Edinburgh and Freedom" Published in *Letters to Israel*).

Particular (vi): Permitted and authorised his wife to act on his behalf in associating with, and making use of, persons known to him to be active in opposing the interests of Great Britain. Among these persons were Anna Wolkoff, Tyler Kent, and Mrs. Christabel Nicholson.

Reply

There is no truth whatever in this Particular; and I propose to treat it with the contempt it deserves.

Needless to say, the Home Office Advisory Committee produced no evidence to support any of the slanders contained in any of the above Particulars

CONCLUSION

I submit this statement, and the comments on the Particulars, not for my own sake, but to enlighten the country.

When things reach a stage wherein a Lord of Appeal, whose papers are suspected of relating to the plan of Organized Jewry, can be "politically burgled";

When a white Paper containing vital passages on Jewish World-Bolshevism can be immediately withdrawn, and reprinted omitting the vital passages;

When a leading British Industrialist can be blackmailed by Organized Jewry, and coerced into submission by boycott, strikes, acts of sabotage and arson;

When a Member of Parliament, who dares to try and warn the country against this menace of Organized Jewry and their help-mates (the only Fifth Column that really exists in this country) is thereupon imprisoned for three years on false charges;

When these things can happen in Britain, then there must surely be something wrong somewhere.

At a time when Britain and the Empire are engaged in a

life-and-death struggle, surely there can be no room for the foul teachings and activities which I have touched upon.

While our sailors, soldiers and airmen are winning victories over the external enemies, surely it is the duty of every patriot to fight this internal enemy at home.

The Prime Minister, in his speech at the Mansion House, stated that he had not become the King's First Minister in order to preside over the liquidation of the British Empire.

There are more ways than one of encompassing the liquidation of the British Empire today; and the National Leder who is determined to counter them all will not only need the utmost support of all patriots, but I believe it will be proved that his most formidable difficulties will emanate from just those very powers which I and other members of the Right Club have all along striven to oppose and expose.

THE STATUTES OF JEWRY

Les Estatutz de la Jeuerie 1275 [A.D.]
From The Statutes of the Realm.
Vol. 1, page 221.

THE STATUTES OF JEWRY[18]

Usury forbidden to the Jews

Forasmuch as the King hath seen that divers evils and the disinheriting of good men of his land have happened by the usuries which the Jews have made in time past, and that divers sins have followed thereupon albeit that he and his ancestors have received much benefit from the Jewish people in all times past, nevertheless, for the honour of God and the common benefit of the people the King hath ordained and established, that from henceforth no Jew shall lend anything at usury either upon land, or upon rent or upon other thing.

And that no usuries shall run in time coming from the

---

[18] The Parliament which passed this Statute included representatives of the Commons, and this was probably the first Statute in the enactment of which the Commons had any part. It is significant that the first evidence of the feelings and wishes of the commoners should have expressed itself in such a form as in these Statues of Jewry, in face of the fact, clearly evident in the script, that the Kings owed much to Jewish activities having demanded monies from the Jews regularly and permitted them in turn to recoup themselves from the people.

feast of St. Edward last past. Notwithstanding the covenants before made shall be observed, saving that the usuries shall cease. But all those who owe debts to Jews upon pledge of moveables shall acquit them between this and Easter; if not they shall be forfeited. And if any Jew shall lend at usury contrary to this Ordinance, the King will not lend his aid, neither by himself or his officers for the recovering of his loan; but will punish him at his discretion for the offence and will do justice to the Christian that he may obtain his pledges again.

Distress for Jews

And that the distress for debts due unto the Jews from henceforth shall not be so grievous but that the moiety of lands and chattels of the Christians shall remain for their maintenance: and that no distress shall be made for a Jewry debt upon the heir of the debtor named in the Jew's deed, nor upon any other person holding the land that was the debtor's before that the debt be put in suit and allowed in court.

Valuing lands taken for a Jew's debt

And if the sheriff or other bailiff by the King's command hath to give Saisin (possession) to a Jew be it one or more, for their debt, the chattels shall be valued by the oaths of good men and be delivered to the Jew or Jews or to their proxy to the amount of the debt; and if the chattels be not sufficient, the lands shalt be extended by the same oath before the delivery of Saisin to the Jew or Jews to each in his due proportion, so that it may be certainly known that the debt is quit, and the Christian may have his land again; saying always to the Christian the moiety of his land and chattels for the maintenance as aforesaid, and the chief mansion.

Warranty to Jews:

And if any moveable hereafter be found in possession of a Jew, and any man shall sue him the Jew shall be allowed his warranty if he may have it; and if not let him answer therefore so that he be not therein otherwise privileged than a Christian.

Abode of Jews

And that all Jews shall dwell in the King's own cities and boroughs where the chests of the chirographs of Jews are wont to be.

Their badge

And that each Jew after he shall be seven years old, shall wear a badge on his outer garment that is to say in the form of two tables joined of yellow felt of the length of six inches and of the breadth of three inches.

Their tax

And that each one, after he shall be twelve years old pay three pence yearly at Easter of tax to the King whose bond-man he is; and this shall hold place as well for a woman as for a man.

Conveyance of land, etc., by Jews

And that no Jew shall have the power to infeoff (take possession of) another whether Jew or Christian of houses, rents, or tenements, that he now hath, nor to alien in any other manner, nor to make acquittance to any Christian of his debt without the special license of the King, until the King shall have otherwise ordained therein.

Privileges of the Jews

And forasmuch as it is the will and sufferance of Holy Church that they may live and be preserved, the King taketh them under his protection, and granteth them his peace; and willeth that they be safely preserved and defended by his sheriffs and other bailiffs and by his liege men, and commandeth that none shall do them harm or damage or wrong in their bodies or in their goods, moveable or immovable, and they shall neither plead nor be impleaded in any court nor be challenged or troubled in any court except in the court of the King whose bondmen they are; and that none shall owe obedience, or service or rent except to the King or his bailiffs in his name unless it be for their dwelling which they now hold by paying rent; saving the right of Holy church.

Intercourse between Jews and Christians

And the King granteth unto them that they may gain their living by lawful merchandise and their labour, and they they may have intercourse with Christians in order to carry on lawful trade by selling and buying. But that no Christian for this cause or any other shall dwell among them. And the King willeth that they shall not by reason of their merchandise be put to lot and soot nor in taxes with the men of the cities and boroughs where they abide; for that they are taxable to the King as his bondmen and to none other but the King.

Holding houses and farms, etc.

Moreover the King granteth unto them that they may buy houses and castilages in the cities and boroughs where they abide, so that they hold them in chief of the King; saving unto the lords of the fee their services due and accustomed. And that they may take and buy farms or land for the term of ten years or less without taking homages or fealties or such sort of obedience from Christians and without having advowsons of churches, and that they may be able to gain their living in the world, if they have not the means of trading or cannot labour; and this licence to take land to farm shall endure to them for fifteen years from this time forward.

A. M. RAMSAY

THE JEWS IN BRITAIN

1215 — Magna Carta

1255 — Ritual murder of St. Hugh of Lincoln. Henry III personally ordered trial and 18 culprits were executed - all Jews.

1275 — The Statute of Jewry passed; confined Jews to certain areas, forbade usury to them and also ownership of land and contact with the people: compelled them to wear a yellow badge.

1290 — Edward I banished the Jews from England.

1657 — Oliver Cromwell, having been financed by Manasseh Ben Israel and Moses Carvajal, allows Jews to return to England, though order of banishment never rescinded by Parliament.[19]

1689 — Amsterdam Jews financed the rebellion against King James II. The chief of these - Solomon Medina -

---

[19] And it has been asserted that the Jews never really left England, but merely went 'underground' until the King was assassinated. That is certainly more plausable than expecting that all Jews LEFT the country. Especially given that Cromwell was a pawn for the Jews, and NOT the King's man.

follows William of Orange to England.

1694 — The Bank of "England" set up and the National Debt instituted, securing for the Jew moneylenders a first charge on the taxes of England for interest on their loans. The right to print money transferred from the Crown to this "Bank of England".

1707 — Economic and political union forced upon Scotland against the vote of every country and borough; the national debt foisted upon Scotland, and the royal mint in Edinburgh suppressed.

FAMOUS MEN ON THE JEWS

Seneca B.C. 4 to A.D. 5

"The customs of this accursed people have grown so strong, that they have spread through every land."

St Justin 116 A.D.

"The Jews were behind all the persecutions of the Christians. They wandered through the country everywhere hating and undermining the Christian faith."

Mohammed 570.

"It is incomprehensible to me, why one has not long ago expelled these death-breathing beasts... are these Jews anything else but devourers of men?"

Martin Luther 1483.

"How the Jews love the book of Esther, which is so suitable to their bloodthirsty, revengeful, murderous appetite and hope. The sun has never shone on such a bloodthirsty and vindictive people, who cherish the idea of murdering and strangling the heathen. No other men under the sun are more greedy than they have been, and always will be, as one can see from their accursed usury.

They console themselves that when their Messiah comes he will collect all the gold and silver in the world and divide it among them."

Clement VIII Pope 1592.

"All the world suffers from the usury of the Jews, their monopolies and deceit. They have brought many unfortunate peoples into a state of poverty, especially farmers, working-class people, and the very poor."

Voltaire 1694.

"The Jews are nothing but an ignorant and barbaric people, which have for a long time combined the most loathsome avarice with the most abominable superstition and inextinguishable hated of all peoples by whom they are tolerated, and through whom they are enriched."

Napoleon

"I decided to improve the Jews: but I do not want any more of them in my Kingdom: indeed, I have done all to prove my scorn of the vilest nation in the world."

Benjamin Franklin 1789.

Statement in the Convention, concerning Jewish Immigration:

"There is a great danger for the United States of America, this great danger is the Jew. Gentlemen, in every land which the Jews have settled, they have depressed the normal level and lowered the degree of commercial honesty.

They have remained apart and unassimilated - they have created a state within a state, and when they are opposed they attempt to strangle the nation financially as in the case of Portugal and Spain.

For more than 1700 years, they have lamented their sorrowful fate - namely, that they were driven out of their motherland, but gentlemen, if the civilized world today should give them back Palestine and their property, they would immediately find pressing reasons for not returning there. Why? Because they are vampires - they cannot live among themselves; they must live among Christians and others who do not belong to their race.

If they are not excluded from the United States by the Constitution, within less than 100 years, they will stream into this country in such numbers they will rule and destroy us and change our form of Government for which we Americans shed our blood and sacrificed life, property and personal freedom.

If the Jews are not excluded, within 200 years our children will be working in the fields to feed the Jews while they remain in the Counting House gleefully rubbing their hands.

I warn you, gentlemen, if you do not exclude the Jews forever, your children's children will curse you in your graves.

Their ideas are not those of Americans even when they have lived among us for ten generations. The leopard cannot change its spots. The Jews are a danger to this land and if they are allowed to enter they will imperil our institutions - they should be excluded by the Constitution."

COPY OF LEAFLET DESIGNED BY THE AUTHOR AFTER THE MUNICH AGREEMENT

Are You Aware that...

MR. CHAMBERLAIN was burnt in Effigy in Moscow as soon as it was known that he had secured Peace, showing very clearly WHO WANTED WAR and who are still working ceaselessly to stir up strife all the world over?

Issued by the MILITANT CHRISTIAN PATRIOTS, 93 Chancery Lane, W.C.1 (Holborn 2137), and printed by W. Whitehead, 22 Lisle st. W.C.2

The Official Gag Reprinted from *Free Britain* June 1954

THE OFFICIAL GAG

Lord Jowitt, either with a belated desire to do Justice to Captain Ramsay or now cautious of repeating he fabrications of the past, has admitted in his memoirs of the War Trials, published in the *London Evening Standard* of May 13th, that the defendants in the Tyler Kent affair were all along acting in good faith.

Lord Jowitt, in order to publish these memoirs at all, has been forced to make a point which neither Captain Ramsay nor Anna Wolkoff are even yet permitted to make in their own defense, the nature of the documents concerned in the case having been declared an Official Secret which they may not divulge.

Others, however, are now free to state what they have

known from the beginning, namely, that Captain Ramsay was never at any time endeavouring to communicate with Germany but was trying to communicate certain information to the then Prime Minister, Mr Chamberlain, which Mr Chamberlain was expecting and which, because of Captain Ramsay's arrest, never reached him.

Something of this information later reached Mr Chamberlain by other channels, however, for it was disclosed in the Forestall Diaries that Mr Chamberlain had become convinced, and actually told Mr Forestall, that powerful Jewish circles in New York were solely responsible for manoeuvring Britain into the war, unsuspected by him at the time although he was Prime Minister and ought to have been informed of what was going on.

The wedge that was driven between Mr Chamberlain and Captain Ramsay was the lock-up and the abuse of the Official Secrets Act, followed by the elaborate dissemination of the complete fabrication by the Home Office that "the said Captain Archibald Maule Ramsay, M.P... had expressed his desire to do-operate with the German Government in the conquest and subsequent government of Great Britain."

Later the Lord Marley added further to this fabrication by stating in the House of Lords that he had it on good authority that Captain Ramsay had agreed to become Gauliter of Scotland under a German occupation of Great Britain. He ignored the challenge of Captain Ramsay's lawyers to repeat the charge outside the House.

For fourteen years Lord Jowitt must have been well aware that Captain Ramsay was conducting an investigation in order to satisfy Mr. Chamberlain that there was documentary evidence for the facts already disclosed to him by Captain Ramsay, and that Captain Ramsay's arrest was made to prevent that documentary evidence from being presented to the Prime Minister. But it has taken all these years for Lord Jowitt to concede that Captain Ramsay is an honest man who "would never have countenanced any act which he recognized as being against the interests of his country."

G.P.

German White Book on the Last Phase of the German-Polish Crisis

From the:

GERMAN WHITE BOOK DOCUMENTS

Concerning the Last Phase of the German-Polish Crisis
GERMAN LIBRARY OF INFORMATION NEW YORK

Note on the German White Book (pp 3-6)

The German White Book, presented herewith, is a collection of official documents and speeches, not a collection of uncontrollable conversations. It does not pretend to cover the entire field of German-Polish relations but, as the title implies, concerns itself solely with the last phase of the German-Polish crisis, from August 4th to September 3rd, 1939.

The Polish-german controversy concerning the Corridor, Upper Silesia and Danzig, began in 1919; it has never, since the signing of the Versailles Treaty, ceased to agitate Europe. For many years intelligent commentators and statesmen of all nations, including Great Britain, agreed that the separation of East Prussia from the Reich and, indeed, the whole Polish settlement, was unjust and fraught with danger.

Germany, again and again, made attempts to solve the differences between the two countries in a friendly spirit. It was only when all negotiations proved vain and Poland joined the encirclement front against Germany, that chancellor Hitler cut the Gordian knot with the sword. It was England that forced the sword into his hand.

Great Britain asserts in her Blue Book and elsewhere that she was compelled to "guaranty" Poland against "aggression" for reason of international morality.

Unfortunately the British Government subsequently admitted (Under-Secretary of State Butler, House of Commons, October 19, 1939) that the "guaranty" was aimed solely against Germany.

It was not valid in case of conflicts with other powers. In other words, the British "guaranty" was merely a link in the British encirclement chain. The Polish crisis was deliberately manufactured by Great Britain with the connivance of Poland: it was the fuse designed to set off the explosion!

Great Britain naturally attempts to becloud this fact. Official British statements on the outbreak of the war place great emphasis on the allegation that England did not give a formal "guaranty" to Poland until March 31, 1939, whereas the German demand on Poland, which Poland rejected, was made on march 21st. Britain contends that the British "guaranty" was merely the consequence of the German demand of March 21st.

Britain denies that her "guaranty" stiffened Polish resistance. She insists that Germany took advantage of a moment of highly strained international tension by springing upon Poland her demand for an extra-territorial road through the Corridor between the Reich and East Prussia.

The British ignore a vital fact in this connection. The existence of the "guaranty", not its formal announcement, was the decisive factor. The future may reveal when the British promise was first dangled before Poland. In any event, Poland was assured of British aid *before* March 21st.

Chamberlain's speech of March 17, 1939, and the statement by Lord Halifax of March 20th, (both reprinted in the British Blue Book) leave no doubt on that question. The British "guaranty" was in the nature of a blank check. Poland did not know when she marched to her doom, that the check would not be honored.

The allegations that the Poles were surprised or overwhelmed by the German proposals, does not hold water. Poland was fully informed of the German demands. When as Herr von Ribbentrop points out in his Danzig speech (October 24, 1939) chancellor Hitler in 1934 concluded a Friendship and Non-Aggression Pact with Marshal Pilsudski, it was clearly understood that the problem of Danzig and the Corridor must be solved sooner or later. Chancellor Hitler hoped that it would be solved within the framework of that instrument.

Poland callously disregarded her obligations under the German-Polish Pact, after the death of Marshal Pilsudski. The persecution of German minorities in Poland, Poland's measures to strangle Danzig economically, the insolent manner the Polish Government chose to adopt with the British blank check in its pocket and the Polish mobilization frustrated chancellor Hitler's desire to settle Polish-German differences by peaceful negotiation, as he had solved every other problem arising from the bankruptcy of statesmanship at Versailles.

No one can affirm that the National Socialist Government did not attempt with extraordinary patience to impress upon Poland the desirability of a prompt and peaceful solution. The Polish Government was familiar with the specific solution proposed by Chancellor Hitler since October 24, 1938. The nature of the German proposals was discussed at least four times between the two governments before March 21, 1939. On October 24, 1938, von Ribbentrop, the German foreign Minister, proposed to the Polish Ambassador, Lipski, four steps to rectify the injustice of Versailles and to eliminate all sources of friction between the two countries.

1). The return of the Free City of Danzig to the Reich, without severance of its economic ties to the Polish State. (The arrangement vouchsafed to Poland free port privileges and extra-territorial access to the harbor.)

2.) An exterritorial [sic] route of communication through the Corridor by rail and motor to reunite Germany and East Prussia.

3.) Mutual recognition by the two States of their frontiers as final and, if necessary, a mutual guaranty of their territories.

4.) The extension of the German-Polish Pact of 1934 from ten to twenty-five years.

On January 5, 1939, Poland's Foreign Minister, Josef Beck, conferred with the German chancellor on the problems involved. At this time Chancellor Hitler offered Beck a clear and definite guaranty covering the

Corridor, on the basis of the four points outlined by von Ribbentrop. The following day, January 6th, at Munich, the German Foreign Minister once more confirmed Germany's willingness to guaranty, not only the Corridor, but all Polish territory.

The generous offer for a settlement along these line, liquidating all friction between the two countries, was reiterated when Foreign Minister von Ribbentrop paid a state visit to Warsaw (January 23rd to 17th, 1939). On that occasion von Ribbentrop again offered a guaranty of the Polish-German boundaries and a final all-inclusive settlement of German-Polish relations.

Under the circumstances it is absurd to allege that Poland was "surprised" by the German proposal of March 21st, and subsequent developments. It is possible that Poland may have concealed Germany's friendly and conciliatory offers from Paris and London. With or without British promptings, Poland prepared the stage for a melodramatic scene, in which the German villain brutally threatened her sovereignty and her independence.

In spite of Polish intransigence, culminating in threats of war, Chancellor Hitler made one more desperate attempt to prevent the conflict. He called for a Polish plenipotentiary to discuss the solution presented in Document 15 of the German White book. This solution envisaged the return of Danzig to the Reich, the protection of Polish and German minorities, a plebiscite in the Corridor under neutral auspices, safeguarding, irrespective of the result, Poland's unimpeded exterritorial access to the sea.

The British are please to describe this reasonable document as an "ultimatum". This is a complete distortion of the facts. The German government, it is true, had set a time-limit (August 30th) for the acceptance of its proposal, but it waited twenty-four hours after its expiration before concluding that the possibilities of diplomatic negotiations had been exhausted. There was ample opportunity for England and Poland to act within those twenty-four hours.

The British take the position that Germany's demands were not known either in Warsaw or London. That pretense is demolished by the British Blue Book itself, for we find here a dispatch from Sir Neville Henderson, the British Ambassador to Berlin, which leaves no doubt that he relayed the German proposal to London after his midnight conference with von Ribbentrop on August 30th, and that he understood the essential points of the German proposal. Henderson even transmitted to the British Government Chancellor Hitler's assurance that the Polish negotiator would be received as a matter of course on terms of complete equality with the courtesy and consideration due to the emissary of a sovereign state.

Henderson sent his night message not only to Downing Street, but also to the British Embassy in Warsaw. There is evidence, which has recently come into the possession of the German Foreign Office that, in spite of all its protestations of ignorance and helplessness, the British Cabinet communicated the substance of Henderson's midnight conversation with the German Foreign Minister directly to the Polish Government. The London Daily Telegraph, in a late edition of August 31st, printed the following statement:

> "At the Cabinet Meeting yesterday, at which the terms of the British Note were approved, it was decided to send a massage to Warsaw, indicating the extent of the latest demands from Berlin for the annexation of territory".

This item appeared only in a few issues. It was suppressed in later editions.

Germany's demands were so reasonable that no sane Polish Government would have dared to reject them. They certainly would have been accepted if England had advised moderation. There was one more chance to preserve peace on September 2nd. It was offered by a message from Premier Mussolini (Document 20). The Italian suggestion was acceptable to Germany and France (Document 21). but was rejected by Great Britain (Document 22).

THE LAST PHASE OF THE GERMAN-POLISH CRISIS

(pp.7-12)

Appended to this are printed the documents which were exchanged during the last days before the beginning of the German defensive action against Poland and the intervention of the western Powers, or which in any other respect refer to these events. These documents, when shortly recapitulated, give the following general survey:

1). At the beginning of August the Reich Government was informed of an exchange of notes between the representative of Poland in Danzig and the Senate of the Free City (Danzig), according to which the Polish Government in the form of a short-term ultimatum and under threat of retaliatory measures had demanded the withdrawal of an alleged order of the Senate — an order which, in fact, had never been issued — concerning the activities of Polish customs inspectors (Documents 1 to 3).

This caused the Reich Government to inform the Polish Government, on August 9th, that a repetition of such demands in the form of an ultimatum would lead to an aggravation of the relations between Germany and Poland, for the consequences of which the Polish government would alone be responsible.

At the same time, the attention of the Polish Government was drawn to the fact that the maintenance of the economic measures adopted by Poland against Danzig would force the Free City to seek other export and import possibilities (Document 4).

The Polish government answered this communication from the Reich Government with an aide-Memoire of August 10th, handed to the German Embassy in Warsaw, which culminated in the statement that Poland would interpret every intervention of the Reich Government in Danzig matters, which might endanger Polish rights and interests there, as an aggressive action (Document 5).

2). On August 22nd, the British Prime Minister, Mr. Neville Chamberlain, acting under the impression of announcements of the impending conclusion of a Non-Aggression Pact between Germany and the U.S.S.R., sent a personal letter to the Fuhrer. Here he expressed on the one hand the firm determination of the British Government to fulfill its pledged obligations to Poland, on the other hand, the view that it was most advisable in the first instance to restore an atmosphere of confidence and then to solve the German-Polish problems through negotiations terminating in a settlement which should be internationally guaranteed (Document 6).

The Fuhrer, in his reply of August 23rd, set forth the *real* causes of the German-Polish crisis.

He referred in particular to the generous proposal made by him in March of this year and stated that the false reports spread by England at that time regarding a German mobilization against Poland, the equally incorrect assertions about Germany's aggressive intentions towards Hungary and Roumania and, finally, the guarantee given by England and France to the Polish Government had encouraged the Polish Government not only to decline the German offer but to let loose a wave of terror against the Germans domiciled in Poland and to strangle Danzig economically. At the same time, the Fuhrer declared that Germany would not let herself be kept back from protecting her vital rights by any methods of intimidation whatsoever (Document 7).

3). Although the above-mentioned letter from the British Prime Minister of August 22nd, as well as speeches made on the subsequent day by British statesmen, showed a complete lack of understanding for the German standpoint, the Fuhrer nevertheless resolved to make a fresh attempt to arrive at an understanding with England.

On August 25th, he received the British Ambassador, once more with complete frankness explained to him his conception of the situation, and communicated to him the main principles of comprehensive and far-sighted agreement between Germany and England which he would offer to the British Government once the problem of Danzig and the Polish Corridor was settled (Document 8).

4). While the British government were discussing the preceding declaration from the Fuhrer, and exchange of letters took place between the French President, M. Daladier, and the Fuhrer. In his answer the Fuhrer again submitted his reasons for Germany's standpoint in the German Polish question and once more repeated his firm decision to regard the present Franco-German frontier as final (Documents 9 and 10).

5). In their answer to the step taken by the Fuhrer on August 25th, which was handed over on the evening of August 28th, the British Government declared themselves prepared to consider the proposal for a revision of Anglo-

German relationships. They further stated that a they had received a definite assurance from the Polish Government that they were prepared to enter into direct discussions with The Reich Government on German-Polish questions.

At the same time they repeated that in their opinions a German-Polish settlement must be safeguarded by international guarantees (Document 11).

Despite grave misgivings arising from the whole of Poland's previous attitude and despite justifiable doubts in a sincere willingness on the part of the Polish Government for a direct settlement, the Fuhrer, in his answer handed to the British Ambassador on the afternoon of August 29th, accepted the British proposal and declared that the Reich Government awaited the arrival of a Polish representative invested with plenipotentiary powers on August 30th. At the same time the Fuhrer announced that the Reich Government would immediately draft proposals for a solution acceptable to them and would, if possible, have these ready for the British Government before the Polish negotiator arrived (Document 12).

6). In the course of August 30th, neither a Polish negotiator with plenipotentiary powers nor any communication from the British Government about steps undertaken by them reached Berlin. On the contrary, it was on this day that the Reich Government were informed of the ordering of a general Polish mobilization (document 13).

Only at midnight did the British Ambassador hand over a new memorandum which, however, failed to disclose any practical progress in the treatment of Polish-German questions and confined itself to a statement that the Fuhrer's answer of the preceding day was to be communicated to the Polish Government and that the British Government considered it impracticable to establish a German-Polish contact so early as on August 30th (Document 14).

7). Although the non-appearance of the Polish negotiator had done away with the conditions under which the British government were to be informed of the Reich government's conception of the basis on which negotiations might be possible, the proposals since formulated by the Reich were none the less communicated and explained in detail to the British Ambassador when he handed over the above- mentioned memorandum.

The Reich Government expected that now at any rate, subsequently to this, a Polish plenipotentiary would be appointed. Instead, the Polish Ambassador in Berlin made a verbal declaration to the Reich Minister for Foreign Affairs on the afternoon of August 31st, to the effect that the Polish Government had been informed in the preceding night by the British government that there was a possibility of direct negotiations between the Reich Government and the Polish Government, and that the Polish Government were favorably considering the British proposal.

When expressly asked by the Reich Minister for Foreign Affairs whether he had the authority to negotiate on the German proposals, the Ambassador stated that he was not entitled to do so, but had merely been instructed to make the foregoing verbal declaration. A further question from the Reich Minister for Foreign Affairs whether he could enter into an objective discussion on the matter was expressly denied by the Ambassador.

8). The Reich Government thus were confronted with the fact that they had spent two days waiting in vain for a Polish plenipotentiary. On the evening of August 31st, they published the German proposals with a short account of the events leading up to them (Document 15).

These proposals were described as unacceptable by Polish broadcast (Document 16).

9). Now that every possibility for a peaceful settlement of the Polish-German crisis was thus exhausted, the Fuhrer saw himself compelled to resist by force the force which the Poles had long employed against Danzig, against the Germans in Poland, and finally, by innumerable violations of the frontier, against Germany.

10). On the evening of September 1st, the Ambassadors of Great Britain and France handed to the Reich Minister for Foreign Affairs two notes couched in the same terms in which they demanded that Germany should withdraw her troops from Polish territory, and declared that if this demand were not conceded, their respective Governments would fulfill their obligations to Poland without further delay (Documents 18 and 19).

11). In order to banish the menace of war, which had come dangerously close in consequence of these two notes, the Duce made a proposal for an armistice and a subsequent conference for the settlement of the German-Polish conflict (Document 20).

The Germans and the French Government replied in the affirmative to this proposal whilst the British Government refused to accept it (Documents 21 and 11).

That this was so was already apparent in the speeches made by the British Prime Minister and the British Secretary of State for Foreign Affairs on the afternoon of September 2nd in the British Houses of Parliament, and a communication to that effect was made to the Reich Minister for Foreign Affairs by the Italian Ambassador on the evening of September 2nd. Thus also in the opinion of the Italian Government the initiative of the Duce had been wrecked by England.

12). On September 3rd, at 9 a.m., the British Ambassador arrived at the German Foreign Office and handed over a note in which the British Government, fixing a time limit of two hours, repeated their demand for a withdrawal of the German troops and, in the event of a refusal, declared themselves to be at war with Germany after this time limit had expired (Document 23).

The British Secretary of State for Foreign Affairs on September 3rd, 1939, at 11:15 a.m. delivered a note to the German Charge d'Affairs in London in which he informed him that a state of war existed between the two countries as from 11 a. m. on September 3rd (Document 24).

On the same day, at 11:30 a.m. the Reich Minister for Foreign Affairs handed to the British Ambassador in Berlin a memorandum from the Reich Government in which the Reich rejected the demands expressed by the British Government in the form of an ultimatum and in which it was proved that the responsibility for the outbreak of war rested solely with the British Government (Document 25).

On the afternoon of September 3rd, the French Ambassador in Berlin called on the Reich Minister for Foreign Affairs and inquired whether the Reich government were in a position to give a satisfactory answer to the question directed to them by the French government in their note of September 1st. The Reich Minister for Foreign Affairs told the Ambassador that after the English and French Notes of September had been handed to him, the Head of the Italian Government had made a new intermediary proposal, to which the Duce had added, the French Government had agreed.

The Reich Government had informed the Duce on the preceding day that they were also prepared to accept the proposal.

The Duce however had informed them later on in the day that his proposal had been wrecked by the intransigent attitude of the British Government.

The British Government several hours previously had presented German with an ultimatum which had been rejected on the German side by a memorandum which he, the Reich Minister for Foreign Affairs, would hand over to the French Ambassador for his information.

Should the attitude of France towards Germany be determined by the same considerations as that of the British Government, the Reich Minister for Foreign Affairs could only regret this fact. Germany had always sought understanding with France.

Should the French Government, despite this fact adopt a hostile attitude towards Germany on account of their obligations towards Poland, the German people would regard this as a totally unjustifiable aggressive war on the part of France against the Reich.

The French Ambassador replied that he understood from the remarks of the Reich Minister for Foreign Affairs that the Reich Government were not in a position to give a satisfactory answer to the French Note of September 1st. Under these circumstances he had the unpleasant task of informing the Reich Government that the French Government were forced to fulfill the obligations which they had entered into towards Poland, from September 3rd at 5 p.m. onwards.

The French Ambassador at the same time handed over a corresponding written communication (CF, Document 26).

The Reich Minister for Foreign Affairs thereupon declared in conclusion the French Government would bear the full responsibility for the suffering which the nations would have to bear if France attacked Germany.

OTHER TITLES

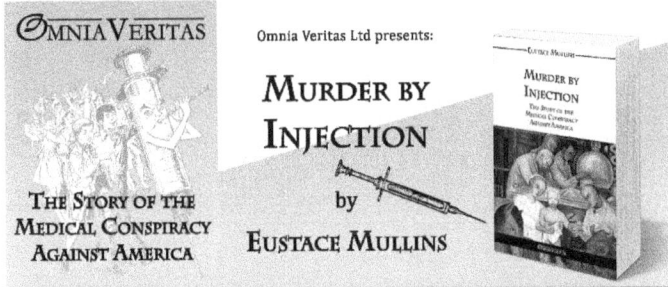

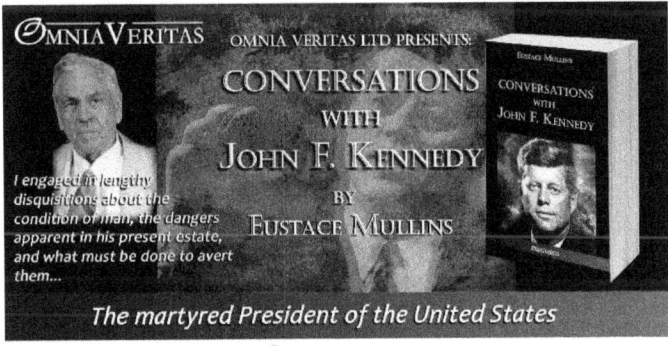

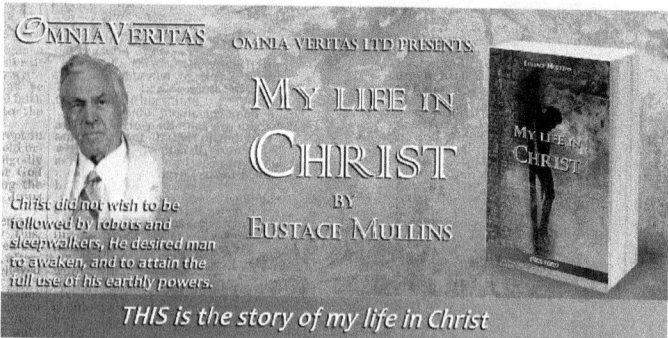

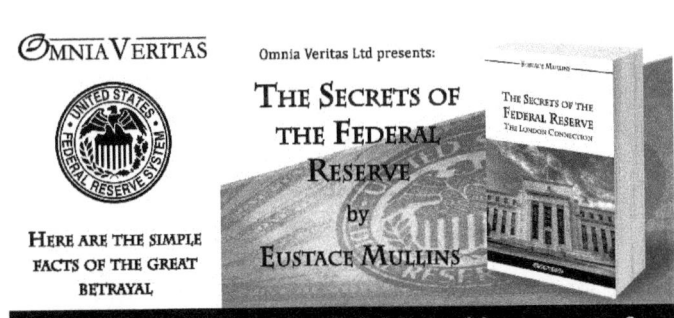

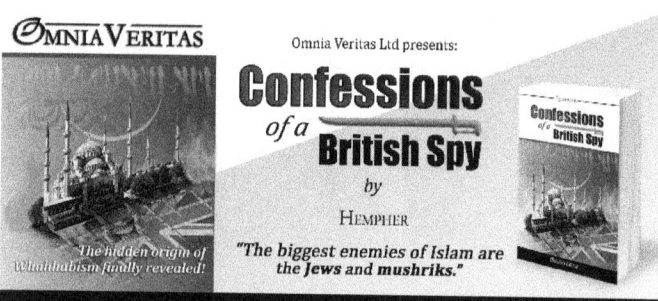

*The **mother** or matron was named from the most **tender** and **sacred** of human functions*

What tender associations halo the names of wife, mother, sister and daughter!

*The time has come for a **book** like this to command the attention of **medical** men...*

... they never learned sex. They never realized its fundamentals...

*... it appears to me that the world is very much as it was-that **Eden** is still possible to those who are fit for it...*

Every man goes to woo in his own way...

Svali Speaks
Breaking Free of Cult Programming

Understand Illuminati Cult Programming

Modern day Illuminism is a philosophy funded by the wealthy

The Art of Kissing

Kisses have been called the balm of love... the nectar of Venus; the pledge of bliss and love; the seal of bliss; the melting sip, and the stamp of love.

When we dwell on the lips of the love we adore, Not a pleasure in nature is missing

THE BLACK GOLD SPIES

by GILLES MUNIER

The story of the series of secret agents who, since Napoleon I and the Great Game, precipitated the collapse of the Ottoman Empire and then obtained control of the world's oil supplies

This saga is akin to an adventure story

OMNIA VERITAS

Omnia Veritas Ltd presents:

The Gentlemen's Book of Etiquette, and Manual of Politeness

A complete guide for a gentleman's conduct in all his relations towards society

BY

CECIL B. HARTLEY

To make your **politeness** part of yourself, inseparable from every action, is the height of **gentlemanly** elegance and finish of **manner**.

As you treat the world, so the world will treat you

OMNIA VERITAS

Omnia Veritas Ltd presents:

The Ladies' Book of Etiquette, and Manual of Politeness

A complete hand book for the use of the lady in polite society

BY

FLORENCE HARTLEY

... to be truly a **lady**, one must carry the **principles** into every circumstance of life

Politeness is goodness of heart put into daily practice

OMNIA VERITAS

Omnia Veritas Ltd presents :

THE NAMELESS WAR

World War II history told by a British war hero.

A first hand testimony of WWII; after reading this book, you'll never look at history the same way again...

An astonishing account of *forbidden history* !

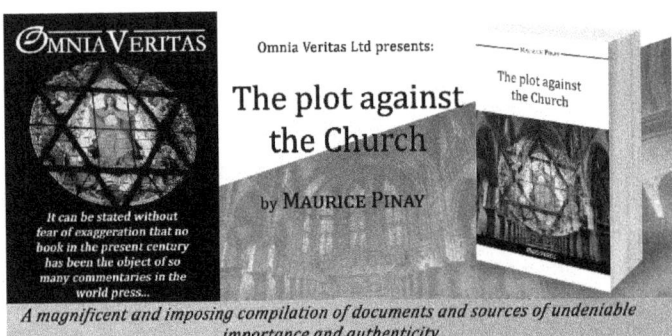
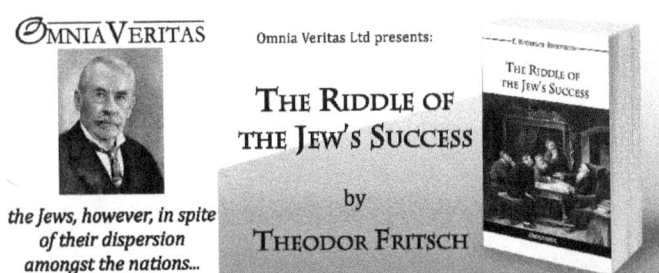
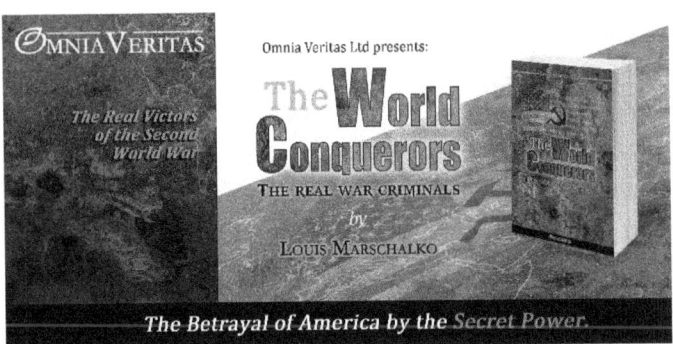

Omnia Veritas Ltd presents:

THE ZIONISTS

by

GEO. W. ARMSTRONG

The fundamental ideology or philosophy of Zionism is that the Jews are the "chosen people"

and that God promised them that they should possess and rule the world...

Omnia Veritas Ltd presents :

The VigilantCitizen
"Symbols Rule The World, Not Words Nor Laws"

ARTICLES COMPILATION

The occult symbolism
in movies & music

To understand the world we live in, we must understand the symbols surrounding us.

The occult references of the entertainment industry !

Omnia Veritas Ltd presents:

Woman, her Sex and Love Life

by WILLIAM J. ROBINSON M.D.

Yes, **love** is a **woman's** whole life. Some **modern women** might object to this...

they will tell you if you enjoy their confidence that they are unhappy...

The life of Napoleon taught by one of the greatest historian of all times!

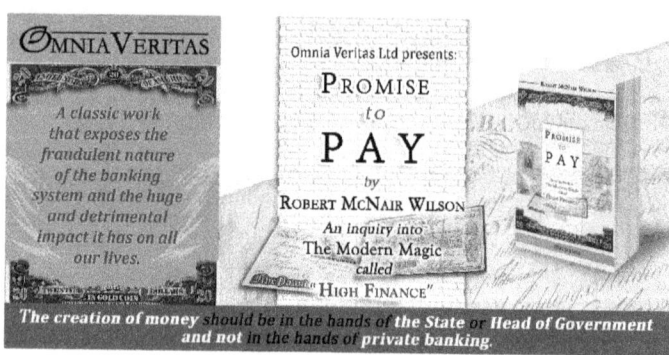

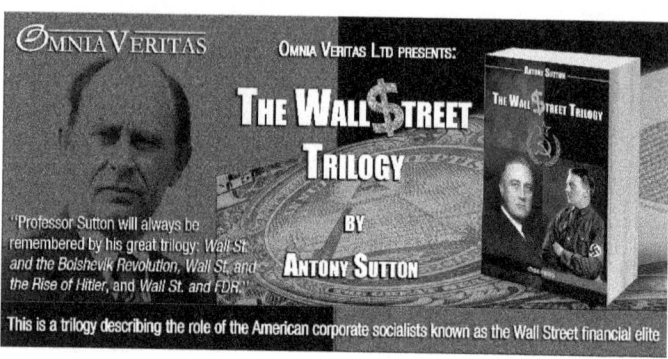

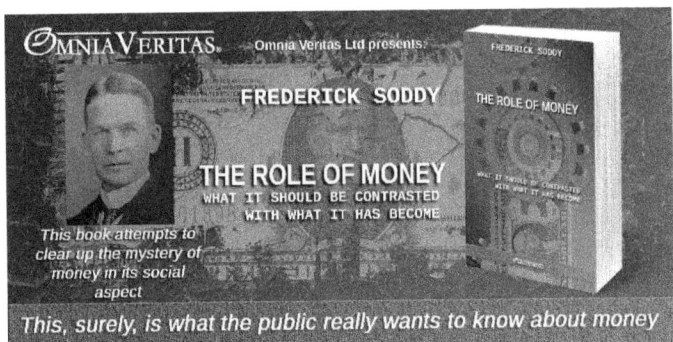